GW00777500

I Should Have Known Better

A life in pop management – The Beatles, Brian Epstein and Elton John

Geoffrey Ellis

THOROGOOD

Thorogood Publishing Ltd
10-12 Rivington Street
London
EC2A 3DU

Telephone: 020 7749 4748
Fax: 020 7729 6110
Email: info@thorogood.ws
Web: www.thorogood.ws

A CIP catalogue record for this book is available
from the British Library.

ISBN 1 85418 219 6

Book designed and typeset by Driftdesign.

For Daniel Martin

Contents

THE AUTHOR SKETCHED BY LIONEL BART C.1966

1
Tomorrow Never Knows

The world changed in the 1960s. Sexual intercourse, wrote the poet Philip Larkin, began in 1963. Youth, it seems, was liberated. Carnaby Street and its flared trousers became the fashion. And the Beatles happened. As for me, I moved from a stable job in New York to exciting, but less secure, work in London, helping to manage the most successful, most famous entertainers in the world. But, for me, the sixties ended in August 1967. The 27th of that month, to be precise. The day Brian Epstein died.

At the time, I was a Director and the Chief Administrator of NEMS Enterprises, the company set up by Brian Epstein a few years earlier specifically to manage the Beatles. I did much of the unglamorous work, running the office, overseeing the staff and, in particular, making use of my legal knowledge by helping Brian to negotiate and conclude the many contracts involved in furthering the careers of the best-known popular performers in the world, as well as those of the many other artistes NEMS was by then managing. I was an old friend of Brian's – a principal reason for my having the job – and after a particularly difficult period, both for Brian and NEMS, he had invited another old friend of his employed by NEMS, Peter Brown, and myself to spend the August Bank Holiday weekend with him at the small country house he had recently bought in Sussex, about fifty miles south of London. The plan was to do very little, simply relax and enjoy a few days in the warm late summer in the country. The Beatles were away in North Wales with the Maharishi, their giggling Indian guru;

Brian was to join them there the following week. Another more recent friend of his, Simon Napier-Bell, himself an up-and-coming manager of pop stars, including The Yardbirds, had also been invited to Sussex, but at the last moment had told Brian that he could not come. Brian was disappointed. He called a contact in London (unknown to me) and suggested that this person could arrange for a few people to come down later that evening to make up something of a party. This arrangement seemed somewhat inconclusive.

Peter Brown and I had arrived late on Friday afternoon and after dinner, served by Brian's recently acquired staff, he announced that he was going to drive himself up to London and seek more company and entertainment. Although we tried hard to dissuade him he was adamant, and left in his convertible Bentley. He said that he would probably spend the night at his London house, in Belgravia, and come back to Sussex in the morning.

A short time after he had left, and somewhat embarrassingly, a London taxi arrived with three or four friends, or rather contacts of the person Brian had called earlier, expecting entertainment at the hands of the Beatles' manager. However, they took his absence in reasonably good part and we were able to rustle up food and drink for the unexpected guests. They later stayed for the night, left in the morning and were never seen or heard of again – by me, at any rate.

Brian did not reappear that morning, but he called to say he felt tired and would probably stay in London until the evening. So Peter Brown and I were left to our own devices, and to enjoy our absent host's hospitality for the whole of that Saturday. It was not for me a particularly agreeable time: Peter Brown and I had never been especially close, and we were both worried about Brian and when he would reappear. He called during the afternoon, apologized for his absence, but said that he would probably stay another night in London.

The next day, Sunday, we received an agitated telephone call from Brian's Italian butler: he and his wife, the cook-housekeeper, were very worried that Brian had not appeared from his bedroom since arriving on Friday evening. Brian's secretary and General Manager, Joanne Newfield and Alistair Taylor, both in London, were summoned to the house, a Doctor, John Gallwey (not Brian's regular doctor, who was away), came in response to an urgent call, the bedroom door was broken down, and Brian was discovered, dead in bed, with several bottles of pills beside him.

Peter Brown and I, who had remained on the phone to the house in London during these events, immediately drove to London. The near two-hour journey gave me time to reflect on how I had come to be involved in the music business and, in particular, in the management of the most famous pop artists in the world; when my upbringing, education or earlier career had by no means prepared me for work of this kind. I did not even like pop music. Nevertheless, I was to become a very senior person in the management organizations of two of the greatest entertainment phenomena of the time, the Beatles and, later on, Elton John.

Nothing in my life before 1964 had presaged my entry into any branch of show business, let alone the business of pop music. I had always been, and remain, a lover of classical music and a devotee in particular of opera. My early life had been fairly conventional for the times: childhood in a middleclass Liverpool suburb; evacuation during the first year of the Second World War to a remote part of North Wales; subsequently, eight reasonably contented and successful years at a Midlands boarding school, Ellesmere College, where my talents were revealed as more academic than sporting; National Service in the Army, wherein I achieved commissioned rank; and three happy years at Oxford, at the end of which I graduated with a degree in law. After leaving university I decided not to pursue a legal career, but to put my knowledge of the law to use in business. Not, however, knowing initially what business to enter, and being unwilling to continue to live off my parents' generosity, I applied for a trainee position in an insurance company, as a stopgap, I thought. However, I found that I liked the work, which was more interesting than I had expected, and I quite rapidly advanced to a position of some responsibility. After a few years I was asked if I had ever thought of working for the company in one of their offices abroad. I had not, but answered that if it were to be somewhere like Paris or New York, I would be interested. Taking to the idea, I studied for a qualification in insurance in French, passed the examination, and was surprised to be shortly afterwards sent to New York.

A friend of my father's had recently married a Czech lady, who enjoyed telling fortunes. She had told me earlier on that my career would be out of the ordinary. I assumed at this time that my moving to America was the fulfilment of her prophecy but much stranger things were to happen in the years to come.

The company I worked for was the Royal Insurance Company, whose head office was in Liverpool; but at the time the most important part of their international operation was in the USA, so it was viewed, not least by me, as a great opportunity for advancement. And I was enthusiastic about moving to New York. In those days – it was 1958 – very few English people had the chance to visit the States, so I was much envied by my circle of friends in Liverpool. I was to travel by ship, the Cunard liner Media, which sailed direct from Liverpool to New York, taking five days for the voyage. Of all my subsequent transatlantic crossings, which over the years have been by propeller aeroplanes, then jet aircraft, from VC10s to 707s to jumbo 747s, to, ultimately, Concorde, the first crossing, by sea, was by far the most enjoyable.

One of the friends who came to see me off at the dockside in Liverpool was Brian Epstein. A few years younger than me, we had become friendly through shared interests in music and in good eating. He had a talent for finding new places to eat, sometimes miles away from the city, and we had many enjoyable jaunts, driving out into the countryside in search of a restaurant that we had heard of or which had been recommended. Brian had had a somewhat troubled education and private life, causing his parents some concern, but had by then apparently settled down, working for his father in the family business, NEMS, the acronym for North End Music Stores, although the shops sold furniture and electrical and household goods as well as radios, television sets and records. At that time, I rather smugly thought that he was pleased to spend time with a friend who had succeeded in getting a good education and who was not tied, as Brian was then, to a family business.

I thoroughly enjoyed my life in New York. I was fortunate to have one or two contacts there, including an English friend from Oxford days who had been living there for a year or two and who was very hospitable and helpful in showing me around the city. My new colleagues, too, were kind, as well as intrigued to have someone from the distant Head Office working alongside them. I soon settled down and acquired a small furnished apartment on Manhattan's East Side, from which it was an easy subway ride to the downtown office, just off Wall Street.

After three years in New York, I was sent for a year to the company's branch office in Chicago. I was glad to see something of the Middle West, although I somewhat missed the New York life. But it was while I was in Chicago that Brian Epstein's parents, Harry and Queenie, came on a visit connected with the furniture business. We had dinner together at their hotel, and I was of course given news of Brian, with whom I had kept in intermittent contact, exchanging occasional letters and greeting cards. He had, it seemed, settled down well in the business, and was in charge of the expanding record department. He appeared, his parents told me, to be content.

After moving to Boston for another year, I returned to New York to take up a management position in the company. It was then that I learned, first in a letter from my mother, that Brian had started to handle the pop group curiously called the Beatles. I then read something of this in the English newspapers that I occasionally bought. In 1963 I spent a few weeks on holiday in England, and naturally heard all about the Beatles from Brian. By then they were famous and I was intrigued to meet one of them, George Harrison: he accompanied Brian and me when we drove out to a country restaurant, although George left us on the way to visit a car dealer who had a car for sale he was interested in buying. He was rather silent, and made little impression on me; no doubt the same was true of any view he had of me. Brain said he was sorry that 'the Boys', as he always referred to the Beatles, were not appearing during my visit to Liverpool, so that I was not able to see them perform. I was perhaps not very sorry.

One evening I was having a drink at the Epstein house when Brian said, not I gathered for the first time, that the Beatles "would be bigger than Elvis". His mother sighed indulgently, and told me when Brian was out of the room that she and Harry were glad that Brian had this great interest, and that his father had agreed to let him have time off work at the stores to allow him to carry out his management duties.

Back in New York, I, and everyone else, started to hear a great deal more about the Beatles, largely due to the publicity efforts of their record company. Stories about their success in Britain and Europe started to appear in the daily press. This alone was unusual, since Americans up until then had no interest in popular music other than that produced and performed in the USA; Elvis Presley was of course the idol of young Americans. I still had little knowledge, or appetite, for popular music, although I had had a surprising experience at a Greenwich Village nightclub, the Bon Soir, which I occasionally patronized. Late one evening, before the advertised act – of which I have no recollection – the compére announced that we were first to hear a young female singer whom they had engaged on the strength of her winning first prize in an amateur talent contest at a largely gay bar round the corner. The audience sighed, having little interest in amateur singers, but when the gawky young woman from Brooklyn began singing everyone looked at each other in surprise, as in a Hollywood movie when an unknown talent bursts on an unsuspecting world. That evening I was present at Barbra Streisand's first professional appearance.

Late in 1963, I received a letter from Brian Epstein, announcing that he was to make his first visit to America, to sound out the prospects of bringing the Beatles to America. I was his only personal friend in New York, so I was pleased at the prospect of showing him around my adoptive home city. When he arrived he was on something of a high. The night before the Beatles had appeared in London, to great acclaim, at the annual Royal Variety Performance attended by Queen Elizabeth the Queen Mother and Princess Margaret. On my recommendation Brian stayed at the Regency Hotel, on Park Avenue, near to my apartment. It turned out not to be an entirely happy choice, as the hotel laundry contrived to lose the pair of gold cufflinks which he had just received from his brother, Clive, as a gift for being best man at Clive's wedding. Brian was accompanied from England by Billy J. Kramer, a good-looking young singer he had just taken under management; he had some idea of promoting Billy's career in America, but in the event he was taken up with arrangements for his major artists, the Beatles. However, one evening the three of us, Brian, Billy and I, were walking through Times Square, when Billy's attention was attracted by a Western-style, tasseled, shirt in a shop window. "No, no, Billy", said Brian, "it's not your style at all." This was the first time I saw Brian exercising his personal manager's influence. Another evening, the two of us went to the Blue Angel nightclub, where the then unknown – at any rate in America – Rolf Harris was appearing. I fancy the sophisticated New York crowd was somewhat bemused by his act, but he was quite enthusiastically received. As for me, I felt that, what with Barbra Streisand and now Rolf Harris, I was seeing something of popular entertainment.

Brian had, during that first New York trip, been making plans for the Beatles to come to America. A few weeks later, the country had been plunged into despair following the assassination of President Kennedy. On that day, Friday the 22nd November 1963, having heard the appalling news while at the office, I went back to my apartment where a friend from England was staying with me; we were undecided whether to accept an invitation to dinner with the future Labour politician and minister, Dr John Gilbert, later Lord Gilbert, and his wife, who were spending time in New York. Although all Americans were in shock and canceling plans, our dinner went ahead, despite our feelings of guilt at enjoying ourselves that evening.

Brian Epstein, too, went ahead with his plans to bring the Beatles to America, and it appeared that the populace was relieved to have something else to think about after a few weeks had gone by. The lamp-posts in New York were plastered with posters announcing the arrival of 'the Boys', and a taxi-driver said to me a day or two before their scheduled arrival "Hey, you're British, you know those Beatles of yours are coming!" The airwaves in New York had been saturated for weeks with their songs, and the local youth had decided that, for once, a non-American act was the tops. This was a little over two months after the assassination of President Kennedy, an event which had left the whole nation traumatized, and the much-heralded arrival of the Beatles was a welcome diversion for young Americans.

They duly arrived, on a day early in February 1964, and were greeted by a mob of teenagers at Idlewild Airport (later, of course, renamed John F. Kennedy Airport) and were swept off to the Plaza Hotel, where they had been booked in by Brian's office simply as Mr Lennon, Mr McCartney, Mr Harrison and Mr Starkey (Ringo Starr's real surname). The hotel did not know what had hit them when crowds of teenagers mobbed all the entrances and screamed for a sight of their new heroes. Brian called me and asked me to come over, meet the Boys and have dinner with him. On arrival at the Plaza, I had no trouble getting through the police lines that had been set up, mostly with mounted police, and getting into the by now heavily guarded main entrance; I was of course no teenager. Brian, who by then had experience of touring with the Beatles, in Britain and in Europe, where they were by then hugely popular, had sensibly booked his own suite on a different floor from theirs, took me to where three of them were sitting and lounging in one bedroom, watching television reports of their arrival, with the sound turned off, and at the same time listening to local stations on portable radios, which seemed to be playing nothing but their songs. From time to time, one or two of them would go to a window and wave to the crowd of youngsters below, who increased the volume of screaming. In a corner, sitting quietly, was Cynthia Lennon, John's wife. Her presence was not publicized – nor indeed was her very existence at that time, since Brian believed that John's popularity with the girls would be jeopardized if it were to be known that he was married. (Somewhat ironic, in view of his later divorce and highly publicized second marriage to Yoko Ono.) I was duly introduced to the three Beatles present and to Cynthia.

The only absentee from the room was George Harrison. He had been taken ill and was in bed, being tended by his sister, Louise, who, married to an American, lived at the time in the mid-west and had naturally come to see her brother and the Beatles' first American appearances. There was some doubt about whether George – whom I had of course already met on my holiday in England – would be well enough to perform the next day. He was and he did.

Before we left the hotel, Brian and I went to his suite, where his publicist, Brian Somerville, was holding the fort and coping with the constantly ringing telephone. He was a large man and clearly had a large appetite as a room service waiter appeared pushing a trolley laden with a substantial dinner. Brian Epstein was not best pleased at the sight of this lavish feast and spoke somewhat testily to Somerville about expenses – my first sight of his occasional sharpness when dealing with his staff. (He and Brian Somerville parted company soon after, and the latter, who had earlier been a naval officer, went on to pursue a successful career as a barrister.) As we were leaving, another of Brian's accompanying staff handed him an envelope bearing the name of the Four Seasons restaurant, then quite new and already renowned as one of New York's finest. The two of us went the few blocks to the Four Seasons in Brian's chauffeured limousine, and on arrival asked the Head Waiter what the envelope, which I noticed bore the name 'The Beatles', was about. It contained, it appeared, an invitation for them to dine there, free, up to an amount of one hundred dollars. Brian thereupon announced that he was the Beatles' manager and that he and his guest would therefore take advantage of the restaurant's hospitality. The management agreed, notwithstanding that the publicity for the Four Seasons would not be quite as great as if the invited guests had attended. Brian then asked me what the equivalent amount in pounds was. I told him that at the current exchange rate it was £42, an unimaginable amount for a dinner for two in London then. We did our best.

Brian gave me a ticket for the Beatles' first American performance, which took place in the venerable and prestigious Carnegie Hall, home of the New York Philharmonic Orchestra. The New York promoter had tried to persuade him to have them play a much larger baseball arena, but Brian had cannily decided on Carnegie Hall, as being certain to sell out and at the same time emphasizing that the Beatles were something very special. Brian, I thus found out early on, always wanted the best for the Beatles. He also wanted the most. Sometime later on, when I was working for him, I asked him how he came up with his enormous demands for appearances in cities all over America. He said that he did everything he could to find out what was the highest fee ever paid at each given venue – very likely that for Elvis Presley – and then simply demanded double. Generally, he got it.

The seats allotted to the friend I took and myself were actually on the stage, among other VIP guests, including the Governor of New

York's wife, Mrs Nelson Rockefeller, and their children. We were therefore behind the Beatles, and thus able to observe the mostly teenage audience who, as became the norm for Beatles' live performances, spent the whole time screaming their heads off. We could not hear a note, but it was an exciting experience for me – and of course for the whole audience.

During that first American visit, the Beatles appeared on the Ed Sullivan Show, then the most popular show on TV. To Brian's annoyance, they did not top the bill, but there was no doubt that they were the main attraction, and the show had the largest audience it had ever achieved. After making an appearance in Washington they returned to Britain but came back to America in August of the same year, 1964, for a longer tour. This time I saw them, courtesy of Brian, at the Forest Hills Tennis Stadium, outside New York City. This of course was an outdoor venue and I was fascinated to observe the entire audience of over 17,000 waving their arms in the air in greeting as The Beatles arrived by helicopter from Manhattan, and saying farewell to them in the same way when they flew off after the show. It was as though they were gods, arriving from the skies for their devotees to pay tribute – which they did, in kind! My friend and I heard not a note, of course. When we were leaving, among the crowd of excited teenagers, some girls heard me talking and shrieked "He's English!" If they had known I was from Liverpool, like their idols, and had moreover actually met the Beatles, I do believe they would have mobbed me.

During the year, Brian made a number of visits to New York, meeting with promoters, lawyers, publishers and record company executives. We always met and I came to know better the darker side of Brian's life. He was, as I knew, gay and had had some minor trouble, briefly involving the police, when living with his family in Liverpool. Now, he was interested in exploring the seamier side of New York's nightlife, visiting gay bars in the notorious Times Square district and even venturing into the wooded areas of Central Park at night, where sexual activity was known to take place in circumstances of great danger. In short, he liked 'rough trade' and reveled in the danger involved. On one occasion, he asked me if I knew of any of the services said to exist for procuring young men. I didn't, but, feeling that there would be less danger to him in meeting and paying for sex than in cruising bars and bushes, I managed to find a phone number for him to call. He did so and arranged for someone who met the specifications he had outlined to come to the Plaza, where he was again staying, that night. Earlier we dined together and he insisted that I accompany him back to the hotel to see that all was well. We found a thoroughly respectable-looking young man waiting outside the door of Brian's suite, and I took my leave. In the morning, I asked him if all had gone well. He replied "Yes, but he didn't really satisfy me, so I went out later and had a good time in the park." Thereafter, I distanced myself from his nocturnal activities.

It was on another of his visits, in the autumn, that he asked if I would be interested in coming to London, where he had recently moved his office from Liverpool, to work for him. He explained that the business was expanding so fast – he had already taken on some more acts for management – that he could not cope alone with the volume of administrative work involved; also, he had come to dislike much of this side of the business and needed someone he could trust to handle most of it. There were, he told me, many people in London who would be only too pleased to work for the Beatles' manager, but he preferred to be surrounded by people he knew and trusted. He had in fact brought a nucleus of employees down from Liverpool with him.

I thought long and hard about Brian's proposal. My career in insurance was going well, and I liked living in America. In addition, I knew nothing about the music business. But it was a fascinating offer to be catapulted into the heart of show business, and in London, which at the time had the reputation of being the heart of the entertainment world. So I said yes. My colleagues thought I was mad, my friends were for the most part envious. At any rate, I prepared to pack up and move back across the Atlantic.

BRIAN EPSTEIN ON HOLIDAY IN VENICE IN THE EARLY 1960s

2
A Day In The Life

The first few weeks of my new employment were spent, not in London, but in New York and Los Angeles. I had agreed with Brian Epstein that it would be useful for me to familiarize myself with what was happening in America for 'the Boys', NEMS Enterprises and the other artists he was managing by then. (As with the Royal Insurance Company, which I had just left, the most important source of income for all these was to be the USA.)

My very first day in my new job provided a complete contrast to my former working days. Instead of taking the subway to the downtown financial district, I walked to the Plaza Hotel, where Brian was ensconced in his usual suite, and had coffee with him while he finished his breakfast. We then went in his chauffeured limousine to the airport and flew first-class to Los Angeles. Two of the NEMS acts, Gerry & The Pacemakers, from Liverpool like the Beatles, and Billy J. Kramer & The Dakotas (Billy I knew from his and Brian's first visit to New York), were contracted to appear on an American TV show and were in Los Angeles to record their segments, as well as to make some live appearances on the West Coast. Brian and I had agreed that it would be useful for me to see how such matters were handled from behind the scenes.

On arrival in Los Angeles, Brian went off to the bungalow booked for him at the Beverly Hills Hotel, while I joined the artists, their road managers and publicist at a more modest, but comfortable, hotel on Hollywood Boulevard. Everyone was most welcoming, whatever they may have thought of this somewhat older (I was thirty-four), definitely squarer, entirely unknown person being landed in their midst. I joined Brian at the Beverly Hills for dinner and he was clearly amused at my being put in this situation. I quite enjoyed it.

The next day, Brian and I went to the studio where Gerry & The Pacemakers were taping their TV performance. For some reason, Gerry was performing his song while sitting in a barber's chair being, apparently, shaved. He acquitted himself well, and indeed Gerry Marsden is still going strong some forty years later. When we left the studio we were surrounded by a group of teenagers demanding Brian's autograph. One or two even asked me for mine; I politely declined.

The same evening I, but not Brian, accompanied Gerry and Billy with their respective backing groups to a gig, which I speedily learned to call a public performance, at an indoor arena in Long Beach, some distance from Los Angeles. Both acts went down well – their Englishness and the association with Brian Epstein and the Beatles no doubt helped – but I was dismayed by the antics of another act on the bill: a young married couple who seemed very amateur to me and, it was clear, to much of the audience. It transpired that it was their first professional live appearance, and Sonny and Cher certainly improved in the months and years to come. Later, divorced, Sonny Bono became a successful politician before his premature death, while Cher is still an elegant, sophisticated solo performer.

On our way back to Los Angeles in the hired bus, I was horrified to see fans of our two groups driving alongside the bus at speed, passing autograph books over and exchanging bottles of Coca-Cola through the bus and car windows. I was also disturbed to find Brian Epstein, when I dropped in at his hotel, smoking pot with a few hangers on. I was assured it was very mild and it did not seem to affect him much. Then.

After those few days on the West Coast, Brian left for London and I returned to New York to spend a few weeks in the offices of Walter Hofer, attorney to Brian Epstein and the Beatles. He was a youngish (my age, in fact) music business lawyer, to whom Brian had been introduced by his client, Dick James, the publisher in London of the Beatles' music. (He actually turned up one day in Walter's office while I was there, on his first visit to the States. We were introduced, but spoke only briefly; I had no idea of his later influence on my life and career.) Walter, whose charming and beautiful wife, Sondra, worked alongside him, was clearly delighted to have these new clients whose fame and success greatly contributed to his own prosperity. It was said that other New York attorneys specializing in the same line of work referred enviously to Walter's gleaming new offices as 'the House the Beatles built'. As well as his secretarial staff, who included Joan Schulman, herself later a music business executive, Walter had a young associate, Robert, or Bob, Casper, also knowledgeable and ambitious, whom I came to know well. In the office suite there was also a room devoted to the Beatles' Fan Club, presided over by a delightful and efficient black lady, Bernice Young. She coped with the huge number of fan letters, asking for autographs, photos or just information about the Beatles – who their girlfriends were, where did they live, when were they coming to America again? For the most part the 'Fan Club Secretary' sent out a polite suggestion that the mostly teenage letter writers join the Fan Club, for a small fee, on receipt of which she issued a package of information and 'signed' photos, i.e. with printed signatures. I doubt if the Club made any sort of profit, but the membership fees helped to cover expenses.

I found, somewhat to my surprise, that there was also a 'Brian Epstein Fan Club'. As I had seen outside the Los Angeles TV studio, he was a popular figure among teenage fans and indeed, good-looking as he was, and the manager of the Beatles and other more or less famous groups, it was hardly surprising that his own publicity in the pop world had resulted in his own fan club. This rather modest outfit both amused him and fed his vanity.

The few weeks I spent in the Hofer office introduced me to a number of figures in the American pop music world. Prominent among them was Norman Weiss, Vice-President of General Artists Corporation, or GAC, the large New York agency that handled all the North American tours by the Beatles and other NEMS artists. It was Norman, an unusually gentlemanly and upright figure in the New York music business, who had seen in Europe a year or so earlier the effect the Beatles had on their audiences. He had in consequence approached Brian Epstein and persuaded him that the time was right for them to try the American market – of course under the aegis of GAC.

Finally, the time came for me to say goodbye to my New York friends, leave my East Side apartment and fly off to London. My airline booking had been made by the NEMS office in London with Pan Am, which was happy to handle all their transatlantic travel business. Gratifyingly, they sent a car and driver to take me to the airport. On arrival at Heathrow Airport, I was met by Alistair Taylor, one of Brian Epstein's Liverpool employees who had decamped with him to London and was now General Manager of NEMS Enterprises Ltd. (It was Alistair who was credited with having been instrumental in sending Brian to see the Beatles in Liverpool's Cavern Club as a result of a customer in the NEMS store's record department persisting in requesting a Beatles record of 'My Bonnie'. Alistair admitted years later that there was an element of myth about this story, there having been no such customer.) On meeting me, he expressed Brian's apologies for not coming to the airport himself as he had a business appointment; however, he had sent his Bentley and driver with Alistair, so my return to England was in some style.

It was a weekend when I arrived in London, and Brian made up for not meeting me by taking me on Sunday as his guest to a 'Midnight Matinee' in aid of charity at the London Palladium. We sat in a box, the third occupant being Lonnie Trimble, Brian's colored manservant; "A treat for Lonnie", Brian said. The star was Judy Garland, with whom Brian had struck up a recent friendship.

Appearing with her was her daughter, Liza Minnelli, then little more than a teenager. She indulged in what I can recall only as a species of 'interpretative dancing', and appeared by no means the sophisticated performer she later became. Brian later gave me a double LP record of that concert as a memento and to mark my starting work with him.

When I arrived at NEMS the Beatles were already preparing for their 1964 Christmas show at the Hammersmith Odeon. I decided I would go and see the show, if only to see whether there was any difference in the behavior of English fans from those in America. A few days earlier I was talking to an old friend from Oxford days, Clement Crisp; he had been my exact contemporary there and was a man of enormous wit and charm. He was also a man of fastidious tastes who had become the erudite ballet critic of the Financial Times. He nevertheless liked the idea of seeing the Beatles in action. We went to the theatre together, in the company's chauffeur-driven limousine, and as we approached it Clement was quite startled to observe the crowds of young fans converging on the entrance, some of them already nearly hysterical with excitement. Clement himself recalls the evening:

"The prospect of seeing the Beatles, then in the first mad flush of their fame, was not to be missed. They were scheduled to give a concert in Hammersmith but we were advised not to turn up for the first part of the evening as this would comprise some insignificant singers for whom the management had no hopes: they were to serve as the thinnest of hors d'oevre. We arrived at the hall – cavernous and filled as far as the eye could see with pubescent girls – just in time for the main attraction. The lights dimmed, a voice (as I recall) announced 'Here they are: the Beatles!' and on to the stage (where drums and a microphone were already placed) ran four young men. Grey suited, mop-haired, they were greeted with screams. Loud, shrill, incessant, and as they mouthed and strummed, not one word or note could be heard. Nor could they for the duration of the concert – or for as long as we remained, since we had to beat a hasty retreat, ears ringing. The girls were

still screaming, the Beatles were still strumming and for all the audience knew were simply miming the words of their songs. This clearly mattered not at all: the fans could see their idols. And the idols, with greatest goodwill, waved and capered."

As for me, I got my confirmation that Beatles' fans were much the same on both sides of the Atlantic.

The first weekend after my arrival in London I went to Liverpool to see my family. Brian said that he too was going to Liverpool then, so of course we traveled together, by train from Euston Station to Lime Street, Liverpool. During the journey we were sitting alone in our first-class compartment when the dining-car attendant came in and asked us if we wanted dinner. We said no, but ordered some drinks. These were brought a few minutes later by a much younger steward, who in handing me my gin and tonic said to me, "Are you Brian Epstein?" I said, "No, but he is", pointing to Brian sitting opposite. "Oh no, you're kidding," was the response, "he's much too young." Brian, whose name was already famous, more so apparently than his face at that time, was very amused: he had considerable vanity and was always extremely smartly dressed, being delighted when he was voted Best Dressed Man by a magazine poll in the mid-sixties. He lived in style too, at that time in a medium-sized modern flat in William Mews, just off Knightsbridge.

At last, on the Monday morning following the Judy Garland show, I arrived at the offices of NEMS Enterprises, which were located on an upper floor of Sutherland House, an undistinguished building next door, as it happened, to the London Palladium, in Argyll Street. I was, understandably I think, nervous about presenting myself at the office for the first time so I was there early. Brian himself was late – a foretaste of his working habits – but Alistair Taylor was there to introduce me to the staff. I had feared that there might be resentment directed at me and my appointment as Chief Administrative Executive, but I swiftly found that this was not the case at all. I was welcomed as someone who had the authority to make decisions and deal with much of the work for which the existing staff was not qualified, or too inexperienced to handle. They were a friendly and enthusiastic bunch. The atmosphere was far more informal than I was accustomed to in insurance offices in England and America. I stuck to my habit of wearing a suit and tie to work, but I was the only one.

There was only one reasonably large office, occupied of course by Brian Epstein; I had to make do at first with a small, pokey office nearby. However, Brian was shortly afterwards to move, with just his personal assistant and secretary, to a more glamorous private office in the heart of Mayfair, ten minutes' walk away, and I inherited his larger, more prestigious space in Sutherland House. The reason for his move was that he had become irritated by the large number of uninvited callers at the NEMS office, these being often aspiring pop musicians, people with unsolicited business propositions for the Beatles, and indeed fans, attracted by the unlikely possibility of encountering their heroes in the offices of their manager. Journalists, too, had become a problem, often besieging the office for stories, photographs and background information. Brian wanted to get away from all this, and no-one outside the company and the artists was to know of his new location. He rather ruined his intention by telephoning all his favorite journalists and other contacts and giving them details of his whereabouts.

There was another small office suite near Covent Garden, which had been NEMS's first London office when the company was still headquartered in Liverpool. This was now occupied by the Beatles' Fan Club, which handled quite efficiently the immense amount of fan mail received from all over the world.

Brian's move to Hille House, as the modern building where his office was located was called, left me in charge of the main center of operations, where I swiftly found that there was much work to be done.

3
Taxman

The time had come for me to become directly involved in various, mostly business, aspects of the Beatles' career. They came, occasionally and irregularly, to Brian Epstein's office for meetings at which he would discuss with them everything which was planned, including future recordings, tours both in the UK and abroad, suggested interviews with journalists, and so forth. Brian always sought "the Boys'" approval before finalising any such arrangements. Their arrival at these meetings presented something of a hazard, as journalists and photographers always seemed to be lurking around when they arrived, and indeed sometimes followed them from their respective homes. For this reason, business meetings with them were not very frequent. (Brian of course saw them quite often privately, individually or together, both socially and to help them with any personal matters.)

The first such business meeting in which I participated followed a discussion which Brian and I had had with Jim Isherwood. He was senior partner in Bryce Hanmer Isherwood, a smallish accountancy firm whose Liverpool office had handled the financial affairs of Brian and the Beatles since the start of their association. Brian had named his company NEMS Enterprises in an act of filial piety to his father's NEMS stores. When he and the company moved to London, Bryce Hanmer Isherwood represented them through their main London office and Jim Isherwood became a close adviser. I was initially somewhat surprised that the same accountants were representing both parties to the artists' management contract, fearing a conflict of interest. But this did not appear to present a problem at the time. Jim Isherwood himself was not in appearance and manner what might be assumed to be the typical accountant: though sporting a smallish moustache, he favoured light-coloured suits and had a very informal manner. He told me that he welcomed my own appointment as he had become concerned at the burden Brian Epstein was bearing, handling all the artistic side of the business and at the same time overseeing the legal, accountancy and administrative affairs of the company and the artists. Jim was indeed very friendly and helpful to me in those early days.

He and Brian had for some time been considering the problems suffered by the Beatles in consequence of the very high rates of taxation in Britain at the time: the top rate of income tax for high earners was 70% (rising a year or two later to 83%, with an additional 15% surcharge on investment, or 'unearned' income, making a total of 98% on much of the income of the richest). The Beatles were earning plenty of money, and the public knew this and expected them to spend and live accordingly. In fact, Brian and Jim limited them to a smallish sum of cash for spending money – abut £200 a week each as I recall – and kept a close watch on their other expenditure, such as that on travel, clothes and servants. The cost of the various flats and houses they acquired was also carefully monitored to ensure that they did not over-extend their resources. After a few years of increasing success, they had virtually no capital or savings.

At this first meeting at which I was present, Jim Isherwood, whom the Beatles by now knew and respected, set out their current financial position and gave an assessment of their earnings and net incomes in the forthcoming months. He indicated the amounts of tax for which they would be liable, and said little more than that we were considering ways of mitigating their exposure to tax. What he said was received more or less in silence. Then George Harrison, normally the most taciturn of the four, said in his deep-voiced Liverpudlian drawl: "Can't you go to Harold Wilson and ask him if he can let us off some tax? After all, we are bringing lots of money into England". There followed an embarrassed silence. Mr Wilson was then Prime Minister of the Labour Government and he had recently met the Boys at a Variety Club luncheon honouring them. They had all got on well and had been photographed together, Mr Wilson being well aware of the political advantage of being seen as a friend of the Beatles. He had no doubt said that he would be glad to help them in their careers in whatever way he could.

Brian broke the silence by saying something along the lines of we would do everything practical to enlist help. I speedily found that George was the most interested in the financial side of their activities, enquiring about earnings, percentages, commissions and so forth. That he felt keenly about his perceived inequities in the tax system was borne out by the words of his song 'Taxman':

> "Let me tell you how it will be,
> There's one for you, nineteen for me.
> Should five per cent appear too small,
> Be thankful I don't take it all."

This meeting was simply to lay out the current position and to assure the Boys that plans were being made to improve their financial position.

Jim Isherwood's first proposal concerned only John Lennon and Paul McCartney, the writers of nearly all the songs the Beatles performed and recorded, and which were thought of by the public as 'the Beatles' songs'. As well as being immensely popular they were already being considered virtually works of art, and were regularly dissected and analysed by writers on music, not only in the pop music press, but also in national newspapers and the serious music publications. One serious music critic and musicologist, William Mann, writing in *The Times* had, succumbing to the general hysteria over the Beatles, described Lennon and McCartney as "the greatest songwriters since Schubert". (Thus, as Colin Welch writing later in The Spectator pointed out, making them superior to Schumann, Brahms, Wolff, Richard Strauss, Reger, Debussy, Faure, Hahn, Duparc, Tchaikovsky and Rachmaninoff, among others.) Whether or not this was the case, it was clear that copyright in the songs was a considerable asset, and it was on this asset that Jim, with the considered approval of tax counsel and other legal advisers, intended to capitalise, to the great benefit of John and Paul. If humanly possible, this was to be achieved before Capital Gains Tax was due to be introduced for the first time a few weeks later.

Copyright in the songs was owned by a company called Northern Songs Limited. This was administered by Dick James through his own company, Dick James Music Limited, often referred to as DJM. The latter had published the first Lennon and McCartney songs to achieve any success, 'Please Please Me' and 'Ask Me Why'. The writers assigned to the publisher ownership of the songs throughout the world for the full period of copyright – which was at the time until fifty years after the death of the composer, or in the case of works written by more than one person, of the last surviving co-writer. The publisher undertook to pay agreed royalties earned by their works to them and their heirs. The royalties agreed in this instance were, again, those usual at the time: 10% of the retail selling price of sheet music sold, 50% of 'mechanical' royalties, that is those received by the publisher from the sales of records and tapes, and 50% from all other income received, including that from abroad, from exploitation of the songs, which might be from their use in films, TV commercials and so on. The contract also recognised that Northern Songs and the writers were each to receive 50% of income from performances, in the case of John and Paul shared equally, this form of income being payable via the Performing Right Society, which collects such income from all over the world. It was then up to the publisher to secure the recordings and other uses of the works to earn as much as possible, to the mutual benefit of composers and publisher alike.

When Dick James realised that Lennon and McCartney's songs were going to be successful – although even he could not have envisaged then how phenomenally successful – he proposed a different structure, of greater benefit to the songwriters than the normal arrangements referred to above. This he hoped would keep them happy with his administration of their future compositions. A new music publishing company, Northern Songs – a name with some small relevance to the Beatles' Liverpool origins – was to be formed, in which DJM would own fifty per cent. (DJM was itself half owned by Dick James, the other half being in the hands of his accountant and close friend, Charles Silver.) The other fifty per cent was broken down as to twenty per cent to be owned by John Lennon, twenty per cent by Paul McCartney and ten per cent by NEMS Enterprises. NEMS would take no management commission from John and Paul's songwriting earnings, its percentage of Northern Songs compensating for the normal twenty-five per cent commission. Northern Songs would enter into an exclusive songwriting contract with John and Paul, whereby all their future compositions were automatically assigned to the new company which would pay them royalties on the lines mentioned above, referred to in the music business as '10/50/50'. These royalty payments were to be made after the deduction of a ten per cent commission from gross income by DJM, justified on the grounds that Northern Songs would have no offices or staff of its own, all the exploitation, royalty payments, accounting and so forth to be carried out by Dick James and his organisation. The directors were to be Dick James, Managing Director, Charles Silver, Chairman, Brian Epstein and Jim Isherwood. (Lennon and McCartney themselves were not at the time considered as directors, since Brian and Jim were to represent their interests.)

These arrangements had been discussed with and accepted by Brian and, on his advice and recommendation, by John and Paul. It was thought to be the first time, in popular music at any rate, that composers had an equity share in the copyright owner which published their own music, and this structure was the prototype of numerous such companies formed, by other publishers as well as Dick James, in the following years. Later still, in the 1970s and 1980s, it became common for songwriters to own their own publishing companies in their entirety, these being only administered by professional publishers for a commission, often of ten per cent or less of gross income; but Northern Songs in the early 1960s led the way to a larger, and fairer, share for songwriters in their own compositions.

The proposal was that in February 1965 twenty-five per cent of the shares in Northern Songs Limited would be sold to the public, the company being thenceforward quoted on the London Stock Exchange. The sale price realised would be received by the existing shareholders in Northern Songs in the proportion of their holdings in the company. Each of the original shareholders, DJM, John, Paul and NEMS, was to sell a quarter of their holding, and the result would be that John and Paul would each receive twenty per cent of the proceeds. If the sale was successful – a foregone conclusion as it appeared – it would net each of them a little under £100,000. This would be free of tax since Capital Gains Tax would not apply until a few weeks later. The amount represented a considerable gain in 1965 and would be the first substantial amount, other than current taxed earnings, received by any of the Beatles.

Although Northern Songs was, by the standards of the Stock Exchange, a very small company and it had traded for only two years, having been formed in February 1963, the Stock Exchange was prepared to admit it, largely on account of its profitability. I was told that normally flotation was permitted only after a minimum of five years' successful trading, and I have no doubt that the rulers of the exchange, the Stock Exchange Council, were influenced by the national, and indeed international, phenomenon which the Beatles had become.

A frenzy of paperwork now ensued, with a series of meetings held at the offices of the solicitors Goodman Derrick and Co, who were advising Northern Songs on the flotation. These were in Bouverie Street, off Fleet Street. Goodman Derrick fielded a team of their lawyers, headed by one of the firm's partners, Alan Leighton Davies; and from time to time the senior partner, Arnold Goodman, would participate. He was a larger than life character, also of considerable physical girth, whose personality seemed to fill the room whenever he was present. Well known for years in professional circles as a leading member of the legal profession, he had recently become famous as the Prime Minister's, Harold Wilson's, solicitor, and he had many other prominent clients. He undertook some extra-legal tasks for the government, including a flight to Rhodesia (now Zimbabwe) in an effort to end that country's illegal independence of Britain. He was ennobled as Lord Goodman and was later appointed Master of University College, Oxford. His interventions in the very detailed Northern Songs discussions were always brief and absolutely to the point. After his death in 1995, one obituarist wrote that Goodman had the ability to cut to the centre of the most tangled web and draw out the essential threads. He certainly displayed this talent in these very complex negotiations.

The other participants in these meetings included Ivor Lewisohn, a partner in the stockbrokers acting in the sale of shares, Jim Isherwood, Dick James, Charles Silver and myself. Brian Epstein did not attend the meetings wherein all the financial, professional and documentary aspects of the flotation were examined in the utmost detail: in the case of the Offer for Sale Document, every penny in the figures was checked and double-checked, and every word and comma examined for its accuracy and relevance. Brian had no taste for such meetings; also, he preferred nearly always not to get into discussions with Dick James, for whom he had increasing impatience. While acknowledging that Dick did an excellent and professional job as the publisher, his assumption of credit for much of the Beatles' success was a constant source of irritation for Brian and for the Beatles themselves. While it would be a natural and normal function for the publisher to attend recording sessions of songs he controlled or was to control, they besought Brian to prevent Dick from visiting the EMI studios while they were recording.

Dick James, originally named Isaac Vapnick, whom I had first met in Walter Hofer's office in New York, was, like Brian Epstein, Jewish. Their respective upbringings, however, could scarcely have been more different: Dick's family were Polish immigrants, his father a butcher in the East End of London, and Dick himself had been a singer, of moderate success, in music-hall before giving up performing – on the grounds of age and baldness – to become a music publisher, at first working for an established publishing house, then branching out independently. His greatest fame as a performer had been achieved as the singer of 'Robin Hood, Robin Hood, Riding Down The Glen', the signature tune of the Robin Hood series on British TV in the 1950s; and he had himself written or co-written a number of songs, including 'I'm a Pink Toothbrush, You're a Blue Toothbrush' for Max Bygraves. He was extremely voluble, and his less successful competitors in the music business sometimes complained that he bored songwriters into such a stupor that they would accept any deal proposed by him just to escape from their meetings with him. But he was a good businessman and had learned a lot from his partner, the accountant Charles Silver, and he was honest. I liked him.

Brian deputed me, in effect, to act at the Goodman Derrick meetings as his alternate as a Northern Songs director, the other three, Jim Isherwood, Dick James and Charles Silver being of course present in person. I was now thrust into negotiations when I knew little of the background as it was only a few weeks since I had joined NEMS. I contrived to hold my own, however, and when asked by Alan Leighton Davies or one of the others some question concerning the Beatles – their forthcoming professional obligations, their recording schedules or the like – it was quite easy for me to find the answers by a telephone call or, at worst, in time for the next meeting.

Finally, the documentation was concluded to everyone's satisfaction. It was necessary for John Lennon and Paul McCartney to sign a number of the papers, including the vital new exclusive songwriting contract with Northern Songs. This replaced the previous one, was to take effect on the day of the Stock Market flotation and gave them an increased royalty percentage of fifty-five per cent in respect of songs to be written thereafter: an extra advantage agreed by Dick James and the others, in addition to the capital gain. (It is worth mentioning here that during all the vicissitudes later experienced by Northern Songs, up to and including its ownership by the American star Michael Jackson, these royalties continue to be paid to Paul McCartney and Yoko Lennon. The many fans and other members of the public who believe that as a result of the company's changes of ownership the composers have been totally deprived of benefit from their songs are mistaken.)

A final signing meeting was accordingly arranged, in the panelled offices at Bouverie Street, over which Arnold Goodman himself presided and which Brian had persuaded John and Paul to attend along with himself. Their signatures were also needed for, among other papers, the agreements to sell part of their own sharehold-ings as well as the new songwriting contract. Alas, a minor error in the contract, possibly a misplaced comma, was found when the signing had already commenced and it had to be withdrawn for re-typing since correction in ink was out of the question. This was before the days of word processors and the fresh paper would take perhaps half an hour to prepare. Both John and Paul said they could not (and did not want to) wait. Arnold Goodman, used to dealing with difficult clients, asked them to stay, but even his powers of persuasion were on this occasion insufficient, and Brian too could not get them to change their minds. They left, leaving the professionals aghast.

In view of the imminence of the planned flotation, only a few days away, arrangements had to be made to convey the retyped document to John and Paul for signature. In John's case, this was relatively easy, since he simply went home. But Paul was leaving that day for a holiday and rest abroad with his girlfriend, the actress Jane Asher, to which he had been looking forward during the previous weeks of recording and live appearances. It was axiomatic among us 'insiders' that his destination could not be revealed, even to professional advisers and publishers, in case of a leak to the press, who would surely descend in droves on Paul in his hideout and ruin his holiday. But the agreement had to be signed, with Paul's signature duly witnessed, and it was essential that someone be present to explain the contract to him and to answer any questions he might have. Paul had gone to Hammamet, in Tunisia, then a little known resort, and the only person available to follow him there was a junior lawyer in Goodman Derrick's office, Brian Clarke. He had participated in the numerous preparatory meetings and was thoroughly familiar with the agreement. He was accordingly sworn to secrecy and followed Paul and Jane on the next available plane, with the precious document in his briefcase. His own signature as witness to Paul's remains on the contract.

Predictably, and despite a few pessimistic warnings by sections of the financial press, the flotation was a success, with the shares rising in value immediately and thereafter consistently until the takeover of the company three years later in 1968. Share applications were received from all over the world, especially from America, many of them for just a few shares from young fans who wanted in this way to 'own' a bit of the Beatles. I myself borrowed some money from my father and made my own modest killing. I also formally became Brian's alternate director of Northern Songs and attended every board meeting in his stead, since he continued in his reluctance to participate in discussions with Dick James and the amount of detail bored him. This was fortunate for me as I enjoyed the board meetings and was able to learn a lot about music publishing. I also quite quickly established a rapport with Dick James and Charles Silver, which was to prove extremely useful to me in the future.

Another early meeting I attended was at the headquarters of EMI Records in their handsome offices in Manchester Square, just off Oxford Street. Brian Epstein had asked me to go with him to a meeting at which he intended to renegotiate the Beatles' recording contract, naturally to the artists' advantage. Despite their tremendous success they were still bound by the original contract entered into when they were unknowns and when indeed Brian had been desperate for virtually any contract. The royalty was a ludicrous one (old) penny per single record sold. Since NEMS took a 25% management fee of the artists' income, with the balance being split four ways, each Beatle ended up with 18.75% of a penny; this, for what was by then the worlds' bestselling recording act. (They did share a 10% holding in NEMS, but that 2.5% share each of the company made virtually no difference to their income.)

Brian was determined to improve their record royalties and indeed he had a strong hand to play. It was said in the business that sales of the Beatles' records were at the time saving EMI Records almost from extinction and, clearly, even if that were an exaggeration, the company would do anything within reason to retain the Beatles and to keep them happy. On the other hand, the Chairman of EMI, Sir Joseph Lockwood, was a tough nut who would not give away anything more than he had to. He was however personally friendly with the Beatles, as he generally was with other pop artists contracted to his company.

We were driven to the EMI offices in Brian's Bentley, Brian admitting to me that it gave him great satisfaction to be arriving in this way to deal with the chairman of the company, in contrast to his earlier seeking a deal from relative underlings at the various record companies – including of course EMI itself – which he had approached with tapes of the Beatles' early performances. (Eventually, as was by then common knowledge, George Martin had taken them on for a subsidiary label of EMI's.)

The meeting took place in EMI's boardroom, where Brian was rather irritated to find that, whereas there were only the two of us on our side of the long table, on the other Sir Joseph sat flanked by six or eight company officials: these included, as well as representatives from the legal and accountancy departments, the heads of the record company, Len Wood and Ron White; also, Sir Joseph's personal assistant, William Cavendish, who became a friend of mine. Brian started out by stating what he wanted a greatly increased royalty rate and a more relaxed attitude on the part of EMI to product commitment, that is, the number of recordings the Beatles were contractually bound to supply in each year. He also requested several additional concessions, including fewer allowable deductions from royalty payments and a substantial increase in income from sales abroad. Sir Joseph, a wily old bird with his genuine paternal interest in the Beatles and in Brian, took note of all that was said and instructed his attendant executives to examine all the financial and contractual implications of our proposals. The meeting broke up with the promise to reconvene when EMI was ready with its response.

This was my first experience, but by no means my last, of the ability of pop artists to demand improvements in their contracts when their success in writing songs and selling records enabled them to, as it were, hold the publisher and record company to ransom; their strength being the threat simply to stop writing songs and recording them unless and until they got a better deal. After all, you can't lock up an artist and force him to write a song.

At the next meeting with EMI Records Brian, feeling that we had been rather outflanked by the EMI side last time, took care to have our accountant, Jim Isherwood, and solicitor, David Jacobs, present and there was considerable discussion of all the tax implications for the Beatles of what was proposed. The discussions with EMI went on for many weeks and even months, with a great deal of correspondence involved – which I myself as a newcomer to the business found fascinating. It happened that when the revised agreement was finally signed I was for some reason not able to be present, but I was pleased to receive a personal note, which read as follows:

"Dear Geoffrey,

This afternoon all the documents concerning Beatles/EMI were finalised and duly completed by all concerned on this side. I am not entirely sure why you were not present at the meeting, but we would all like to acknowledge that you had a great deal to do with this matter and that your co-operation and help during negotiations was greatly appreciated.

Yours sincerely,

Brian"

4
With A Little Help From My Friends

I soon settled into the NEMS Enterprises office and swiftly became familiar with my new colleagues, all of them enthusiastic and committed, and for the most part, unlike me, devoted fans of the Beatles and, to a greater or lesser extent, of the other acts by then managed by Brian Epstein. Among the prominent staff were two I had already met: Alistair Taylor, General Manager, who had met me at Heathrow Airport on my arrival, and Tony Barrow, Head of Press and Public Relations, who had been among the team I encountered in Los Angeles when he accompanied the two groups on their West Coast tour. Tony was an experienced and friendly expert in keeping the press hounds happy and himself drafting and issuing press releases about the Beatles' activities. There was also Bernard Lee, the hard-working booking agent who had learned his trade with the Grades and who now negotiated and arranged all the appearances, live and on television, of the NEMS artists other than the Beatles; he generally had no difficulty securing dates for the acts we managed, but his life was made more difficult by the fact that many of the promoters he dealt with hoped that by offering NEMS artists favorable terms they could then secure the Beatles for future appearances. There was no chance of this, Brian Epstein himself being the only one who could contract the Beatles. There was also John Lyndon, in charge of presentations, that is staging the acts, wherever they were appearing.

A vital member of the team was the head telephonist, Laurie McCaffrey, an original member of Brian's staff from Liverpool. She was always under pressure, and quite unflappable. She needed to be, as there were constant calls from all over the world to 'the Beatles' office', all of which she dealt with calmly and efficiently. Also, since this was before the days of reliable direct dialing overseas, she handled very many out-going calls for all of us. I found out later that when Brian was on one of his frequent foreign trips all I would need to say to her was "Get me Mr Epstein, please", and she would do it immediately, knowing at all times where he was and the relevant telephone number.

The whole team, including secretaries, book-keepers and other office staff, were, though not particularly highly paid – Brian's ideas on this score were for some time based on Liverpool rather than London costs – immensely dedicated and hard-working. It helped that they were the envy of so many, friends, families and showbiz associates, and that they themselves basked in the warm glow of association with the Beatles.

Also frequently in the office were the Beatles' own two most important employees, their road managers, Neil Aspinall and Mal Evans. Neil, a former trainee accountant, was an old friend of the Beatles, particularly of John Lennon; Mal, a gentle giant, was expert at shielding the Boys from fans and hangers-on as well as at organizing their travel and preparations for their live appearances when on tour. Neil Aspinall eventually became the head of the Beatles' Apple organization and a jealous guardian of their rights, while Mal was accidentally killed years later in California.

And then there was Wendy Hanson, Brian Epstein's Personal Assistant. I had first encountered her in New York when she organized my tickets to the Beatles' first USA concert in Carnegie Hall. At that time she gave me the impression that she was far too busy and important to concern herself with such a minor matter.

However, very soon after we started working together in London we became fast friends. She was a tall, glamorous, thirtyish blonde, from a prominent Yorkshire business family. She had left England for America while still in her early twenties, and her first job was as secretary to the elderly conductor, Leopold Stokowski; he was famously difficult, but Wendy was highly efficient and secured his confidence, and eventually friendship. Later, she worked as assistant to the Italian-American composer, Gian-Carlo Menotti; he, as well as writing operas such as 'Amahl and the Night Visitors' and 'The Consul', founded the Festival Dei Due Mondi in Spoleto, Italy. It was while working with him there that she fell in love with Italy and all things Italian. This led her to later buy a small house in Tuscany where she intended eventually to retire permanently. After leaving Menotti she had been freelancing for a record company in New York when she was recommended to Brian Epstein because he found on an early visit that he needed help in organizing his business affairs there. Although her experience had up until then all been in classical music, which she loved, she and Brian hit it off immediately, and she soon accepted his offer to work for him full time and, like myself, relocate to London. This was only a short time before my own arrival at NEMS. We swiftly became friends and allies.

Wendy necessarily saw quite a lot of the Beatles, especially when she traveled with them and Brian on tour, and they too came to like and respect her. She was always well groomed and efficient, and I believe they liked her partly because of the contrast she displayed with the often scruffy and outwardly disorganized personnel who surrounded them in their professional lives.

Among others I met at the NEMS offices were different artists who were by then managed by Brian Epstein. Apart from Gerry & The Pacemakers and Billy J. Kramer & The Dakotas, the most prominent was undoubtedly Miss Priscilla Maria Veronica White. She had been a cloakroom attendant at the Cavern Club in Liverpool when the

Beatles were appearing there, and had impressed Brian with her considerable talents as a singer. So he took her under management and changed her name to Cilla Black. She had a string of hits and has had the greatest and most enduring success of all his artists, barring the Beatles, being now, forty years on, reputed to be the highest paid performer on British television.

Cilla's relations with Brian were frequently stormy as she from time to time accused him, probably rightly, of treating her as secondary to the Beatles. They would however kiss and make up, and Brian would promise that she would always have a special place as his only female artist. Even in the early days, Cilla could be imperious, conscious of her status as a star. Wendy Hanson recalled wryly that, when Brian asked her to accompany Cilla to New York for a short cabaret season at the Plaza Hotel, Cilla ordered her to carry her bags from the taxi into the hotel, a chore that was not to Wendy's taste. They did not really get on, but Brian, who arrived a day or two later in time for Cilla's opening night, smoothed things over between them. Wendy took to pronouncing a hard 'C' in Cilla, though not I fancy to her face.

5
Here, There And Everywhere

As well as dealing with contracts, tax matters and various company administrative affairs, there were concerns over aspects of the Beatles' lives which required attention. The secrecy over Paul's whereabouts when he went on holiday, awkwardly for the preparations for the Northern Songs stock market flotation, was typical of the discretion which always had to be exercised over the movements of each of the four Beatles, and over all aspects of their private lives. The Press and Public Relations functions of NEMS Enterprises were exercised in two contrasting directions: Tony Barrow and the assistant who joined him sometime after I came into the picture, Keith Howell, had to operate in two opposing ways so far as their Beatles-related activities were concerned. On the one hand, they had to issue information by way of press releases and personal contacts with journalists about the Boys' professional activities. They had likewise to ensure to the best of their abilities that published information concerning tours, broadcasts, record releases and so forth was accurate – a difficult task, as I would soon realise, after reading endless stories in the music press and elsewhere which were simply made up and bore no relation to the facts.

On the other hand, Tony, Keith and everyone else at NEMS who might have knowledge of the Beatles' private lives and activities, including myself, had to exercise the utmost discretion when asked by outsiders about any such details. Brian Epstein, too, who generally enjoyed his contacts with the press and got great pleasure in making announcements about the Beatles' and sometimes his own plans, was totally discreet about their private lives and activities.

Ringo was going to get married, his fiancée being a nice girl from Liverpool, Maureen Cox, formerly a hairdresser. It was common knowledge that they had been engaged for sometime and they were clearly in love. Some snide sophisticates in London had sniggered at their insistence on always sitting side by side when with others in restaurants or at dinner in friends' houses. When the date for their wedding was decided on, in February 1965, Brian helped to plan the affair like a military operation. I was particularly intrigued by the detail that even the name of the London Hotel where Maureen's parents, Mr and Mrs Cox, were to stay when they came from Liverpool for the wedding, was kept a secret: the press were not to know even this. More important for the newlyweds' happiness was maintaining secrecy over their honeymoon destination, and it was a fact that the newspapers had reporters waiting at stations and airports to try to find out where they would be heading, the West Indies being the favorite bet. The actual honeymoon venue was far less exotic: after the civil ceremony at Caxton Hall, London, at which Brian was best man, Ringo and his bride drove down to the quiet South Coast resort of Hove, which in the winter particularly is lacking in any glamour and is lived in mainly by a retired middle-class population. Brian's friend and lawyer, David Jacobs, had a house there which he used as a weekend retreat and he had kindly offered it to Ringo for a few days. The press were well and truly flummoxed. In fact, the house, which I visited several times myself as a guest of David Jacobs, was surprisingly glamorous inside. Behind a typically suburban exterior, David had had a rear extension built which was all white wood and mirrored glass, with a long bar taking up the whole of one wall. He entertained his show business friends and clients there a great deal. For the new Mrs Starkey it was a not inappropriate foretaste of her future surroundings and lifestyle.

During 1965 I became more directly involved in the activities of the Beatles. Their first film, 'A Hard Day's Night', had been a smash hit, and the American production company, United Artists, was anxious to follow it up. In view of the Beatles' increased fees for the second film, Jim Isherwood had devised a scheme to protect, at least in part, their film income from the excesses of British taxation. A vital ingredient of this was that much of the new film, 'Help!', should be shot abroad. This was agreed, and the Bahamas and Austria were the chosen locations. A former partner of Bryce Hanmer Isherwood, Dr Walter Strach, had recently taken up residence in Nassau, Bahamas, principally to assist in schemes involving offshore earnings of the firm's clients, and his help was sought for the Beatles. An entirely legal scheme was devised which involved substantial amounts of the Beatles' earnings from the film being paid to an account over which they had in fact no personal control, the money being held in trust for them. I was personally rather dubious about this, but everyone else, Brian included, was content with the arrangements, which in the event resulted in no loss to the Boys.

When the filming moved to Austria I accompanied Brian, the Beatles and the film people on the special plane to Salzburg, which had been chartered by the production company. There Brian and I occupied a large, two-bedroomed suite in the best hotel with stunning views on the Austrian Alps. It is true that most filming involves, principally it seems, endless waiting around on the part of the actors and everyone else, apart from the technicians. During some of the waiting time on location I fell into conversation with the actress Eleanor Bron who was appearing in 'Help!', and we agreed that it was a great pity that the filming schedule did not permit us time to leave the area where the shooting was taking place for long enough to visit the Mozarteum in Salzburg. I could have gone by myself but it would have been more fun with her. I was reminded of this agreeable encounter when, some years later, I spent a few months working with Eleanor Bron's brother, a music publisher in London for whose father Dick James had worked with after ceasing to be a singer. Small world, especially in show business.

I visited the 'Help!' filming once again with Brian after the production returned to Twickenham Studios, just outside London. We took some LP records which Brian had promised the director of the film, Richard Lester. They were in the boot of the Bentley, and when Brian's chauffeur took them out and handed them to Dick Lester he eyed the car and said "Thanks very much, but I'd rather keep the package they came in". It was Dick Lester's innovative style of filming the Beatles running and jumping during performances of their songs in 'A Hard Day's Night' that, widely imitated, started the sophisticated style of performances which became common. Another first, set by and around the Beatles.

In the studio they were filming a scene in 'Help!' which involved Ringo traveling in a lift. This had been specially constructed on the set and Ringo got in and out of it more times than I could count until the scene was satisfactorily in the can. There was once again much waiting about and boredom. Filming is not much fun.

Around the same time I paid my first visit to the EMI Studios where the Beatles were recording – as it happened, the song 'Help!'. Their producer, George Martin, was in control. Whereas the finished recording of a pop song may last for only three or four minutes, recording it can take many hours, and it certainly did for the Beatles. On this occasion I was there for about an hour and a half, during which the song must have been performed – and taped – at least a dozen times. Often the positioning of the microphones had to be altered, or the actual performance by one or more of the Beatles was unsatisfactory, either to George Martin or to John Lennon, who was the leader, certainly on this particular recording. Finally, it seemed that everything was just right, with a perfect performance. But George Martin demanded that they take a rest and do it again, since by that time, he said, they had lost their freshness and attack. I left them to it, realizing again the demands and time that successful performance, of both films and records, requires.

I came to know and like both George Martin and his wife Judy. He had been a salaried producer on the staff of EMI Records when he signed the Beatles and started producing their records. When they became a huge success and the mainstay of EMI he was still on his staff salary, so he asked for a share in the income from the Beatles' recordings. This was refused and he decided to leave, but with the knowledge, confirmed by Brian and the Boys, that they would retain him and no one else as their producer for all future recordings. As an independent producer, then a rarity, he was now able to negotiate the percentage which he required from his former employers. George shortly afterwards set up a production company together with three other successful record producers, who likewise left their former positions as employees of record companies. He thereby set a precedent for record producers, who today frequently enjoy percentages not dissimilar from those paid to the recording artists themselves. As with the setting up of Northern Songs, the handling of the Beatles' affairs paved the way for greater rewards for the artistic, as opposed to the administrative, side of the business.

Despite his devotion to the production of the Beatles' recordings, to which he contributed so vastly, and in spite of his genuine liking and admiration for them as people and musicians, George Martin occasionally became exasperated at their behavior, particularly when they were late for recording sessions or when they ignored – for a time – his advice. Once, over a convivial lunch, which happened to follow a frustrating session with the Boys, he burst out to me "Sometimes, when a reporter asks me for a quote on what the Beatles are really like, I'm tempted to answer: they're still the same stupid arrogant bastards they always were". But this was a very rare outburst. For the most part, they made an excellent team of five in the studio.

GEOFFREY ELLIS CHATS TO GEORGE HARRISON IN THE NEMS OFFICE, WHILE JOHN LENNON LOOKS OUT OF THE WINDOW

A vast amount of fan mail for the Beatles was received at the NEMS offices and it was sometimes difficult to sort out genuine business letters from the sacks of mail delivered nearly everyday. As well as letters obviously addressed by kids to the Beatles or to an individual Beatle, some fan letters were disguised as business letters, typically, and most often from America, by having typed envelopes addressed to Mr Brian Epstein, the contents being a request to pass on an enclosed envelope to the desired recipient. All fan letters were passed over to the dedicated Fan Club staff in their separate, scruffy office about a mile away from NEMS. Fan mail virtually never reached the Beatles, but the Fan Club sent out material to correspondents which included photographs of the Beatles either with overprinted signatures or, I regret to say, signatures forged by various members of NEMS's and the Fan Club's staff, some of whom became quite expert at this task. Those fans who joined the Club, as with its American counterpart, were charged a small subscription which did not cover the full cost of the operation; the net cost was charged to the Beatles as a promotional expense.

Occasionally, a random selection of a few fan letters, which came from all over the world, was brought to me to read. Even more occasionally, I took some action as a result of comments by a writer. An instance was a letter – I think there was more than one in similar vein – from a fan in America protesting at the sale there of post-card sized photos of the Beatles sitting and standing on the Stars and Stripes. This, it seemed, was an insult to the flag (and certainly would not have been allowed in the States). I took the trouble to write back, apologizing on the Beatles' behalf and assuring the writer that no offence had been intended. Presumably, the photograph had been taken with some idea of emphasizing the closeness and affection the Boys felt for America.

Sometimes mistakes were made in sorting the mail. In the spring of 1965 one of the NEMS staff came into my office in a late afternoon with four brown envelopes, one each addressed to Mr John Lennon, Mr Paul McCartney, Mr George Harrison and Mr Richard Starkey. These had been thought to be fan mail and had languished for a few weeks in a sack of letters waiting to be taken over to the fan club. However, someone had spotted that they looked like official letters, similar to those from the Income Tax authorities. In fact, they contained identical letters from the Prime Minister's office informing each of the Beatles that Her Majesty The Queen had been graciously pleased to accept the Prime Minister's recommendation that she should confer on him membership of the most honorable Order of the British Empire; in other words, make each one an MBE. The letters requested acknowledgement to 10 Downing Street with acceptance or otherwise by a date which I noted to my dismay was the next day.

The Beatles were still busy in the EMI recording studios in Abbey Road and it was an article of faith at NEMS – in fact Brian Epstein's strict instructions – that they were not to be interrupted for any reason while recording. Brian himself was out of town at the time, but I decided that this needed prompt action and had someone take the letters over to the studio right away. I heard nothing further that day, and knew that, since they nearly always worked far into the night, the boys would probably not get to the studio and start work until the next afternoon. I spent that day in suspense until the acknowledgements of the prime ministerial letters came back to me, duly signed by John, Paul, George and Ringo. I dropped everything else and drove straight to 10 Downing Street, about two miles away through rush hour traffic. I was able to drive right up to the doorway of the Prime Minister's residence (the iron gates at the opening of the street from Whitehall were only installed about twenty years later against the threat of IRA bombs) and handed in the Beatles' acceptances just before the deadline.

The awards, initially to be kept secret, were duly announced in the Queen's Birthday Honors in June. The announcement created a predictable furore, and the Beatles subsequently received their insignia at an investiture by the Queen at Buckingham Palace amid immense publicity, most, though not all, of it approving. Brian was disappointed, as he confessed to me and other intimates, that he was not honored himself and was not consoled by Paul McCartney's labored joke, later repeated to Brian by Princess Margaret, that in this case MBE stood for Mister Brian Epstein.

Brian had indeed become something of a celebrity. He decided that the modern flat he lived in was no longer suitable and bought an early nineteenth century house in Chapel Street, Belgravia. He engaged a fashionable decorator, Kenneth Partridge, to give it an elegant period look and greatly enjoyed buying suitable antique furniture, and choosing fabrics and color schemes. The result was a remarkably attractive interior in which he installed a Spanish couple, Antonio and Maria, as butler, always in black coat, and cook. His chauffeur, always in uniform when on duty, lived not far away and tended the maroon Rolls Royce limousine with darkened windows for which Brian had exchanged the Bentley. The L-shaped drawing room on the first floor was particularly elegant, with an eighteenth century portrait of a lady holding a peach on the wall facing the fireplace, and two full-length windows overlooking the street. The 'L' part of the room had fitted bookshelves and, the house being at the end of a row, a side window looking on to the entrance to the mews at the rear. The room was comfortable too, with chairs and sofas placed for easy conversation.

Brian loved to entertain in the house, and one of his first parties was given for the trumpeter Herb Alpert and his Tijuana Brass group. These big, brash American musicians seemed quite overawed by the splendor of this private home and impressed by Brian's own elegance and charm. They were also impressed by the presence of the Beatles. Another occasion I remember was a dinner party for six, three of the guests being Sir David Webster, the General Administrator of the Royal Opera House, Covent Garden (an old acquaintance of both Brian and myself from the time when he had been General Manager of the Liverpool Philharmonic Orchestra), the lawyer David Jacobs and myself. Brian decided that we needed some younger faces as well, so invited two others, one of whom – I forget the other – was Tommy Nutter, who was just starting out as a tailor independently; he soon became quite a star of the Sixties, dressing pop stars and actors as well as the rich and fashionable in his Savile Row premises.

Some months later, George Harrison married Pattie Boyd, a ravishingly pretty model whom he had first met on the set of 'A Hard Day's Night', in which she appeared as an extra. Brian gave a dinner party at Chapel Street for them after their wedding at which the other guests were Paul McCartney and his girlfriend Jane Asher, George and Judy Martin, Wendy Hanson and myself. Paul had been the only other Beatle to attend the wedding. After the usual excellent dinner, and over coffee and brandy in the drawing room, we played some silly word games, one of which involved each person confessing what his or her idea of heaven was. I forget most of the responses, including my own, but two stay in my memory: Brian's, who said that heaven for him would be having a record at number one in the charts all the time (which I thought rather sad); and George's, who simply said "Having a lot of sex, all the time". Pattie blushed prettily.

Brian's relaxation was not all at home. From time to time, following our practice of long ago, he and I would seek out a new restaurant to sample, not always in the West End, but sometimes out of the center in, say, Hampstead or Islington. A passion of his was gambling and he became a well-known figure in London's fashionable casinos and gaming-houses. Very occasionally I accompanied him, but this would only be for the preceding dinner which we would enjoy: at

Crockford's, then in Carlton House Terrace, and at the elegant Clermont Club in its William Kent house in Berkeley Square above Annabel's night-club, we would dine sumptuously without a bill being presented, Brian being a valued client in the gaming rooms, before he ascended to try his luck at roulette and the other games of chance. I would soon slip away as gambling holds no attraction for me.

Occasionally, Brian's reputation could cause embarrassment. We were dining together once in the Mirabelle restaurant, a favorite of his, when the late film star, Laurence Harvey, who had been dining noisily in a large party at a table close by, lurched past on his way to the door saying loudly to his companions while looking at Brian "I didn't know they let queers in here nowadays". This was a few years before the legalizing of homosexuality between consenting adults, and although London society and show business was generally quite tolerant, such boorishness was sometimes apparent. On this occasion it came particularly ill from Laurence Harvey, whose own sexuality was said to be ambivalent. Brian was unfazed.

When Brian became well-known, I once asked him if he had ever considered changing his name from Brian Samuel Epstein. All I had in mind was that he might have wished to avoid any anti-Semitic prejudice in his progress to success and fame. He was horrified and said that it had never crossed his mind; and there is probably less prejudice of this sort in show business, and many very successful impresarios, producers and agents are Jewish, the most notable example being the Grades (although they did change their name, from Winogradski). Brian did not in fact suffer from anti-Semitism and was proud of his fairly orthodox background, although not himself regularly practising his religion.

There is no doubt that Brian felt a great attraction for John Lennon. John was of course aware of this and would tease Brian about his homosexuality, sometimes cruelly. The story has been related elsewhere of how, when Brian was preparing his somewhat premature autobiography in 1964, he asked the Beatles what they thought he should call it. 'Queer Jew', John shot back. (Brian eventually settled on 'A Cellarful of Noise', referring to his discovery of the Beatles in the Cavern Club in Liverpool; 'A Cellarful of Boys', another wag, this time not John Lennon, called it.) Personally, I discount the stories of a physical relationship between them. Brian was too shy, especially with John, to take such an initiative himself, and John was assertively heterosexual.

I did not particularly like John Lennon. I realize that saying so may well incur the wrath – possibly leading to book burning – of the thousands upon thousands of fans who, particularly since his murder in 1980, have virtually deified him. I admire his work – his song writing, especially of the songs he wrote with Paul McCartney, and to some extent his authorship and draughtsmanship – although I think his simple line drawings are the work of a very minor talent indeed. But his scorn of the fans, his sharp tongue and his conscious nurturing of his 'working-class hero' image, despite coming from a respectable lower-middle-class background, made him into a figure which I found deeply unsympathetic. He was, to use an overworked phrase, too clever for his own good, as he no doubt found out when he made his famous remark about the Beatles being "more popular than Jesus". Although the statement was misunderstood, particularly in America, it proved damaging and could have been disastrous. He should have known better.

John's treatment of his first wife, Cynthia, was in my view unkind and eventually beyond a doubt ungenerous. She was pushed into the background from the start. When I first met her, in the Plaza Hotel suite in New York on the Beatles' first American trip, she was being kept behind the scenes, since Brian had persuaded John that to reveal publicly at that stage that he was married would put the teenage fans off him. John could have resisted this, since by then the Beatles' popularity was so immense that virtually nothing could have damaged them; and there were after all three other Beatles, all of them then single. (Possibly, Brian was also influenced by his feelings for John and didn't like him being married.) Cynthia's presence on that American visit was an exception. I liked the shy, vulnerable Cynthia, who happened to share the same birthday as me. She was generally left at home while the Beatles were on tour, leaving John free to womanize along with the others. When they finally divorced, leaving John free to marry Yoko Ono, Cynthia received a reported settlement of £100,000, no vast sum for a Beatle by then. Following John's death, his widow Yoko continues to receive the income from the songs he wrote and recordings he made when married to her – generally of lesser quality than the Lennon and McCartney songs and Beatle recordings – and also, much more lucratively, all John's shares of royalties from all the earlier works, written and recorded, while Cynthia was John's long-suffering wife. Yoko is as a result said to be one of the richest women in America. Life, as well as John, seems to have been unfair to Cynthia.

As to John and Yoko's posturing for peace, in and out of bags, these seem to me to have been frankly ludicrous.

John Lennon was never rude to me, or to my knowledge spiteful about me, notwithstanding that I was one of the 'suits' whom as a group he despised. Indeed, on one occasion he was, as we shall see, distinctly sympathetic to me. But I cannot overcome my distaste for his memory. I found my opinion somewhat vindicated by John's and Cynthia's son, Julian, who has enjoyed a moderately successful career as a pop artist himself. In an interview published in the Daily Telegraph in May, 1998, he expressed his opinion that his father was a hypocrite who could talk out loud about peace and love but was unable to show it to his wife Cynthia or to himself.

To revert to Brian, his London life was outwardly respectable, and he had become a well-known man-about–town, sought after by hostesses and admired for his style and charm as well as for his good looks. He was seeking at this time to extend his interests beyond management of the Beatles. Indeed, even before I joined him at NEMS he had several acts under contract: as well as Gerry and the Pacemakers, Billy J. Kramer and the Dakotas and Cilla Black, all of whom were from Liverpool and were stars in Britain, there were Cliff Bennett and the Rebel Rousers, The Fourmost, Sounds Incorporated, Michael Haslam, The Big Three, Tommy Quickly (borne Quigley) and Paddy, Klaus and Gibson. There were also, for a short period, the Moody Blues; although a star group already, their period with NEMS was not happy on either side. All these acts were signed up with a good deal of fanfare, with Brian proclaiming his devotion to the interests of each one. Naturally, they all hoped that his magic touch would transform them into stars of the Beatles' magnitude. Clearly this was impossible, even if NEMS had been a much larger, more professional organization, and if Brian had devoted as much time and effort to each act as he did to the Beatles – an absolute impossibility. So a few acts fell by the wayside, and the others for the most part jogged along, with at least the aura of Brian Epstein as their nominal manager to comfort them. Brian himself eventually realized this, and that other members of the hard-pressed NEMS staff were themselves carrying out most of the functions of the personal management which were nominally his. When, therefore, he contracted an unknown folk group called 'The Silkie', his last signing, he specifically named Alistair Taylor as their personal manager rather than himself. Alistair was delighted and carried out his functions with an enthusiasm that was not matched by much success for the group.

Exceptions to the general rule were Gerry Marsden and Billy Kramer (William Howard Ashton to his family and friends). Gerry, to this day, maintains a punishing schedule of performances worldwide, mostly on the international cabaret circuit, and is a rich man.

Brian did not make life easier for himself by the way he lived. Discounting even the problems he made for himself by his homosexuality, and his resultant guilt feelings at concealing this wherever possible, his late night gambling and socializing resulted in increasing unreliability in business activity. His private office in Hille House, Stafford Street, near Bond Street and Piccadilly, was organized by Wendy Hanson, his Personal Assistant, and his secretary, Joanne Newfield. Wendy's own secretary, also installed in Hille House, was Jody Haines; she had come to the notice of Brian and the Boys by being one of the 'Carnation Girls', two fans who turned up with carnations at as many Beatles' concerts as possible and politely handed them in. Joanne Newfield later married the Bee Gee's drummer, Colin Petersen, and moved with him to Australia. Wendy, Joanne and Jody formed an intensely loyal team to Brian which covered up for him as far as humanly possible, making excuses when he was late, sometimes for important appointments and, increasingly frequently, when he did not turn up at all.

On one of my own first visits to Hille House for a meeting with Brian and Jim Isherwood we were discussing, as so often, the Beatles' tax affairs when a messenger arrived with an acetate from the EMI studios, where the boys had been recording the test pressing of the final version of a new single record, 'Yesterday'. Brian, who of course had heard the song many times during the sessions, insisted on playing it for the three of us to listen to. He pointed out that it was the first time a quartet of classical string players had performed as backing musicians on any pop record. I genuinely liked it – still do – despite not being an uncritical fan of all the Beatles' music. So did Jim, and we both made obvious comments to the effect that it would no doubt do well. How well I don't think even Brian could have envisaged then. Quite apart from the popularity of the Beatles' own recording, it swiftly became the most 'covered', that is, performed and recorded by other singers, record of all pop songs. It is also the most performed work in the USA controlled by BMI (Broadcast Music

Inc), one of the two major royalty-collecting organizations in America. In 1989, BMI presented Paul McCartney with a special award to mark an estimated five million performances in America. BMI's executives traveled to Paul's home for this purpose as he could not attend the luncheon in London, at which I was present, when Yoko Ono graciously accepted John's award for his share in the song, widely known to have been largely composed by Paul alone. However, in the days before the split, it had been agreed between them that they would share jointly the credit and the royalty income from all their songs. Many of them were in fact genuinely joint compositions. Then, in late 1993, I was at a dinner at the Dorchester Hotel in London given by BMI at which 'Yesterday' was honored for six million American performances. This time Paul did attend with his then wife Linda to receive his award, and I told him I hoped I would be around to see him get something for the ten millionth performance.

I always Paul found very agreeable, and he can indeed be charming and co-operative. Wendy Hanson, who spent some time on tour with the Beatles, found him what she termed a typical Gemini; that is, charming and difficult by turns. He had displayed his willful side when he left the country on holiday when he was needed in Goodman Derrick's office in London to sign the Northern Songs flotation papers. He can be waspish, too. When he visited the PRS offices where I was working in the early 1990s, he charmed the delighted clerical workers by posing for snapshots with them; but when I recommended him on that occasion to read Ray Coleman's recently published biography of Brian Epstein, saying that it was a serious book "not just sex, drugs and rock'n'roll", he riposted "But that's just what Brian's life was". Now of course Sir Paul, he conducts his life with commendable discretion and relative modesty, despite being the ultimate pop multi-millionaire. It is a curious fact that when he married his first wife, the American Linda Eastman, many people in the press and elsewhere, knowing of her monied background, assumed that she was a member of the family that founded Eastman Kodak. Not a bit of it: her father, a prominent New York music business attorney, had changed his family's name – from Epstein.

6
Eight Days A Week

The Beatles had by now conquered much of the world – that part of it at any rate where records were sold, for pop tours are generally planned to include territories where record sales by the artists involved can best be encouraged. They had even been successful in France, up until then the country most resistant to British and American talent. But they had not been back to Germany since their pre-Brian Epstein days in Hamburg, when they had been an unknown act of four wild boys appearing at the Star Club in the Reeperbahn, living – and living it up – in squalid digs with, it was said, a regular flow of girlfriends. After Brian took on their management, cleaned up them and their act, and when they had as a result become the most sought-after act in the world, they had appeared in most Western European countries, but not in Germany. German promoters were puzzled and clamoured for their return there. The reason for the long delay in doing so was not hard to find: paternity suits. Several German girls had, since the Beatles became famous, launched claims that a Beatle had fathered their illegitimate children in the Hamburg days. Although there would be legal complications, and considerable expense, for such claims to be pursued by German girls in England, writs could be served on any putative father if he set foot in Germany. This was the sort of publicity which neither Brian nor the boys themselves wanted. So our London lawyers, David Jacobs's firm of M.A. Jacobs and Son, became involved in lengthy negotiations with a number of lawyers in Germany. Since Brian saw

Germany as a potentially lucrative market and the Beatles longed to return in triumph to the country where they had, as it were, cut their artistic teeth, the patrimony suits had to be disposed of. David Jacobs consulted with me over these claims and eventually they were settled on fairly reasonable terms. Liability was denied; money changed hands; a total ban on any claims made in public was imposed. And the Beatles could journey into Germany without fear of children being produced as their bastards. There was some nervousness when the time came for the long-postponed tour to start, but all went well.

These paternity claims were not confined to Germany. One day an attractive young Englishwoman of the 'Sloane Ranger' type appeared in my office stating that John Lennon was the father of her baby. Unless she was given financial satisfaction she was, she said, quite prepared to give – or rather sell – her story to the press. She was well spoken, clearly well educated and determined. Our hard-pressed lawyers were called into play once more, and nothing more was heard of the young lady and her alleged half-Lennon child.

I went to Munich myself in the spring of 1966, a few weeks before the German tour, which was in fact at the start of the Beatles' last world tour, to finalise the contract with officials of 'Bravo' magazine, the promoters of the German segment. In their offices I had the unnerving experience of sitting in a chair discussing the finer points of the deal while a photographer silently circled round me taking a great many photographs. Next morning, the Munich paper carried a head and shoulders shot of me with a story describing how Herr 'George Ellis' had come to Munich to sign the contracts for the Beatles to come back, at last, to Germany. Even the German press, it seems, never gets everything right.

At this time, Brian Epstein was taking a short holiday in Madrid, one of his favourite cities, and he asked me to visit him there on my way back to London to report on the German negotiations. (As it happened, the only way to do this, according to our travel agents, was to go back from Munich to Heathrow and catch a plane to Madrid, so it was hardly 'on the way back' from Munich.) When I arrived, and had unpacked in my bedroom in Brian's suite, I reported on the German tour contracts and arrangements. Everything was fine and Brian announced that he had tickets for us to attend the corrida the next day. I told him that I didn't like bullfights: I had seen one, said to have been a good one as it was attended by the Caudillo, General Franco, while I was on holiday in La Coruna in the 1950s and had been sickened by the cruelty to bulls and horses alike. Brian's face fell, as bullfights were a passion with him, and he told me that this was the week of the San Isidro festival, when the finest fighters and the finest bulls competed. Also, the tickets had been expensive and hard to obtain. Weakly, I gave in and spent much of the next day sitting in a huge crowd of aficionados, in the hot sun and with my eyes closed for much of the time. (I thought of the last queen of Spain, until the current restoration, Queen Victoria's granddaughter Queen Ena, who when obliged to attend a bullfight raised to her eyes a special pair of binoculars when a kill was imminent: the lenses were blacked out.)

I had been able to escape a similar experience the year before, when Brian had rented a villa for a few weeks near Marbella, on the Costa del Sol. I flew down to join his house party there for a weekend. (On the plane from London a chatty woman in the next seat, after extracting from me some personal details in the way some strangers on planes do, asked me if Brian Epstein was queer. This was still in the relatively censorious 1960s, and in my reply I was economical with the truth.) Among my fellow guests was Lionel Bart, then at the height of his fame as the writer of the musical 'Oliver'. Brian told us all that he had chartered a plane to fly himself and four others to Seville the next day to go to the bullfights there. Two people had to stay behind, so it was easy for me to opt out. Lionel, too, said he would be happier staying behind, so he and I spent a lazy day on the beach. We had lunch at one of the beach restaurants, ate quite well and drank a lot of wine. We both caught the sun while dozing in the afternoon, but all the same talked a lot. On the way up to the house Lionel offered me a job to administer his business affairs, which were at the time rapidly expanding. (I saw him on the beach at Fire Island, near New York, a year or two later, when he took my breath away by telling me of his then current dollar income alone. Later on, things were not always so favourable for him.) I was flattered, but declined the job, saying I was happy with what I was doing.

Brian's passion for bullfighting led him to form a business associ-ation with a bullfighter. The English critic and writer Ken Tynan, who was also an aficionado and knowledgeable about the so-called sport, introduced him to a young Englishman, somewhat improbably named Henry Higgins, who had achieved a modest success in the bull-ring and was becoming quite well-known in Spain, principally because of his nationality. Brian agreed to manage him, and I resignedly drew up the contract. It provided for advance payments to Mr Higgins, but resulted in no income for NEMS.

Brian enjoyed summoning his senior employees to report to him in person when he was holidaying abroad. For one thing, he could not leave his business behind him: it followed him everywhere, by post, telephone and visitors; and for another, he genuinely enjoyed enter-taining those who were close to him in more relaxed surroundings than was ever possible in London. Thus, once while he was staying at the Cap-Estel, a favourite hotel of his in Eze-bord-de-Mer, on the French Riviera, he asked Wendy Hanson to come down from London for a couple of days to discuss outstanding matters and at the same time to enjoy the change of scene in this very luxurious hotel. Then I was to go down for the weekend. I arrived and went to Brian's room just as he was finishing up his correspondence with Wendy. She took my waiting taxi to Nice Airport and I moved into her room while the chambermaid was still changing the sheets and making the room ready for me. Two things stand out in my memory from that weekend. First, I paid my only visit to the Casino in Monte Carlo, where Brian lost a fair amount of money. And, secondly, we lunched one day with an Englishman called David Shaw, who was holidaying on a yacht nearby and was said to be a financial genius, making his name in the City of London. He struck me then as a nervous character, highly intelligent, who was clearly interested in the finances of the Beatles and Brian Epstein. The occasion was social and the conversation general. But the contact with Mr Shaw was to have very considerable repercussions.

A project in which Brian took a keen interest, on his own behalf as well as that of the Beatles, was participation in a bid to take over one of the independent television franchises in the United Kingdom. He had been approached to join a group of financiers and TV producers who were putting together a bid to take over the franchise currently held by Southern TV. Brian was genuinely enthused about this project and had secured the Beatles' agreement, not only to their own financial participation if the bid were successful, but to an undertaking to appear in a limited number of programmes for the new company. Naturally, the other participants in the consortium hoped and believed that the inclusion of the Beatles in their plans would be a persuasive factor in the eyes of the Independent Television Authority, the ITA, as the controlling body of the independent TV network was then known.

When the detailed work of preparing the submission to the ITA started, I was naturally thrown into the fray, deputising for Brian at the lengthy and complex meetings of the parties involved. There were budgets (and contributions thereto) to be discussed and agreed, production plans to be mapped out, personnel to be approached – some in great secrecy as they were currently working for putative competitors – and the immensely detailed submission to be drafted, argued over and finalised; it had to be a combination of the possible and the attractive.

Brian did however attend the actual interview at the ITA's headquarters in Knightsbridge, although to the general disappointment the Beatles did not. (Actually, I shuddered to think of the disruption to the very businesslike proceedings that their presence would have caused.) The various groups of applicants were interviewed in turn by the board of ITA and our group was scheduled to be seen at 4.30 p.m., following I believe the existing Southern TV group, seeking to have its franchise extended. Our chairman was Viscount de Lisle, an immense grandee, VC, Knight of the Garter, aristocrat and establishment member par excellence. I and some others were in considerable awe of him. I had thought initially that he had been co-opted as a mere figurehead chairman. I was swiftly disabused at our earlier meetings: a director or chairman of a number of City companies, he had an impressive grasp of facts and figures, was genuinely and personally interested in the success of the submission – his stately home, Penshurst Place, was in the Southern TV area – and his presentation of the submission was lucid and thorough. (The detailed written submission had of course been read and considered by the ITA in advance of the interview process.)

The Chairman of the ITA, Lord Hill, was a complete contrast to Lord de Lisle. A medical man by profession, he had made his name as Dr Charles Hill, the 'Radio Doctor', broadcasting on health matters during the Second World War. Trading on his broadcasting reputation and his Northern bluntness and accent, he had gone on to make a career in broadcasting administration. (Ennobled by Harold Wilson, he later changed sides from the ITA, being appointed by Wilson as Chairman of the BBC.)

Our group had been kept waiting until later than 4.30pm and when we entered the ITA boardroom Lord Hill, with no more than a cursory acknowledgement of our presence, demanded of his office staff tea for himself and his half-dozen colleagues. None was offered to us, the absence of this elementary courtesy being astonishing to Brian, myself and no doubt the others. Lord de Lisle led our presentation eloquently and professionally, and the production and financial experts followed. There were few questions from the Board and we were dismissed, again with no particular courtesy. We lost the bid, although we were told we had come near to unseating the incumbents. It was not a very pleasant experience.

There were some lighter moments. A French art dealer had for some time been pestering Brian and me about a picture that he had and which he was sure one of the Beatles, or Brian himself, would be interested in seeing, with a view of course to its purchase. This sort of thing happened quite often and for the most part we were able to put such people off. I tried my best, but the dealer – I cannot remember his name but will call him Monsieur Dupont – was very persistent; one day he called to say he had brought the picture, a Modigliani, to London and invited Brian and myself for lunch the next day at Claridges, where he was staying, in order to see it. It chanced that we were both free that lunchtime, so we accepted.

An acquaintance of mine at the time was David Carritt, the well-known art expert. He had made his name when still very young by discovering and authenticating valuable paintings, mostly old masters, for owners unaware of their value. Recently, for instance, he had discovered that the painted ceiling of the main reception room at the Egyptian Embassy in South Audley Street, Mayfair, was by the Venetian artist, Tiepolo. The embassy had had it removed and sold for an enormous amount, replacing it with a copy. All this had generated a lot of press publicity and David Carritt was retained at the time by Christie's, the fine art auctioneers. He also undertook private commissions. I telephoned him after accepting Monsieur Dupont's invitation and he agreed to accompany us to Claridges the next day. Monsieur Dupont accepted this arrangement, so I called round to Christie's to pick up David in the morning. I found him in his office there negotiating with an alarmingly handsome young Latin

American who had a pair of earrings which he wished Christie's to sell. (I never found out precisely why David was handling this transaction as jewellery was not his field. Later, I learned that Christie's suspected that the young man had appropriated the ear-rings from his mother without her knowing; they declined the sale.) David, an exotic character, was trying on the earrings himself and suggested that the Latin American accompany us to lunch. I had no option but to agree, since David had said that out of friendship he would not charge us a fee for his opinion of the Modigliani; lunch was to be sufficient.

Brian had already arrived at Claridges when the three of us arrived, and Monsieur Dupont was polite enough to accept the addition to his lunch party, which took place in his suite. The picture was standing on an easel, covered by a cloth, while we were I supposed softened up by a good lunch and excellent wine. During coffee and brandy the dealer removed the cloth, revealing the painting. It seemed to me to be a rather typical Modigliani portrait and the reason for its hoped-for purchase by a Beatle was clearly that the subject had a haircut just like the Boys then sported, which was still uncommon in England. Monsieur Dupont extolled the painting's qualities, named his price and expressed his willingness for David Carritt to examine it as closely as he wished. David thereupon proved his worth by whipping out a magnifying glass and looking carefully at every square inch of the painting. At the conclusion of his scrutiny he stated that it was a genuine, if unremarkable, Modigliani, pointed out that the subject was a girl – however much her hair resembled a Beatle cut – and said that on the open market it was probably worth a little more than half what Monsieur Dupont was asking. Brian indicated politely that he could not recommend the Beatles to buy it, nor was he interested himself. Monsieur took it all in remarkably good part and we all left. Brian invited the young South American to dinner.

One of my chores was to see aspiring clients of NEMS Enterprises, that is, pop artists who applied to be 'managed by Brian Epstein', which they thought at this time would be the key to worldwide success. There was virtually no hope of any such applicant being accepted since it was only Brian himself who chose those he wanted to manage, not the other way round. So it fell to me to see those aspirants who were determined enough to get past the barrier of discouragement for preliminary interviews. One of these was the young Jonathan King, the university-educated singer-songwriter who had just had a great success with the song 'Everyone's Gone to the Moon'. I duly reported on my meeting to Brian but he wasn't interested. Jonathan King went on to build a successful career without the Epstein management as a disc jockey, writer, producer, self-publicist and all-round extrovert – until he fell foul of the law in matters unrelated to his music.

On another occasion I had a visit from an old Oxford acquaintance, Derek Bowman, who surprised me by telling me that he had a management arrangement with an up-and-coming pop singer by the name of David Essex. He was seeking an association with NEMS to help him with the large amount of administrative work which entailed. Again, this was not acceptable and David Essex went on to achieve stardom without our help.

One day, a telephone call was referred to me: it was from a very persistent person who wanted to speak to Brian, or preferably to one of the Beatles. Naturally, this was impossible, since the caller was unknown to anyone at NEMS and would not state what his business was. Finally, I spoke to him and found out that he had an American accent and that he was carrying, he said, 'something for the Beatles'. It seemed to be typical of numerous calls from people, often young fans, who would try anything to get near the Beatles, simply to meet them and obtain their autographs. However, this young man sounded quite serious, even though he would not say what it was he had for them, merely that he had come thousands of miles to give it to them.

Eventually I relented, saying I could spare him five minutes myself later that afternoon, and he consented to come and see me in order no doubt to persuade me to contact the Beatles on his behalf.

At the appointed time he turned up and introduced himself, although I don't remember his name. He was Canadian, from Vancouver on the west coast, he told me. He looked the typical American college boy of the time, well scrubbed with short fair hair, clean well-pressed chino pants and trainers. He was very polite, but at first refused to tell me his proposed business with the Beatles, or what he had for them. When I assured him that there was no chance of getting any further unless he told me his business he finally gave up and said "I've got a lot of LSD for them". I was horrified, LSD being the drug that was 'fashionable' at the time in some pop music circles, but was known to be very dangerous indeed, often inducing among other things suicidal tendencies. Concealing my feelings, I asked the young man to explain. He told me he had been approached by some men in Vancouver, where he was a college student, with the proposal that he should carry a substantial amount of the drug to London. Obviously, those who made this suggestion were banking on the fact that he had a wholly innocent appearance, and in the event he had passed unchallenged through customs. He had accepted without, I fancied, wholly realising the enormity of what he was doing, although he did know it was illegal. He had been induced to become a carrier by the promise of the jet flight to England; he had not flown before or left North America. He had also been given enough money to cover his accommodation and living expenses, but I gathered there had been no question of any substantial payment to him. He was clearly an amateur. The Canadian supplier or suppliers had told him the Beatles were likely purchasers of the LSD, doubtless basing their belief on current speculation in some quarters, including some of the tabloid press and music papers, that some of their recent songs, especially 'Lucy in the Sky with Diamonds' (L...S...D) were influenced by drugs. He had got hold of the telephone number of NEMS Enterprises – there was nothing secret about it – and here he was.

I was in a quandary. On the one hand, detesting drugs myself and being unwilling, to say the least, to connive at any breaking of the law, I wanted to stop my visitor from peddling his package of LSD anywhere; certainly not to the Beatles. On the other hand, it appeared that the only way I could ensure that he was caught with his load would be to ask him where he was staying and how he could be contacted, thus opening up the possibility that he would say to anyone that "the Beatles are interested and are going to get in touch with me". With the press always snooping around the office the likelihood of any resultant publicity was alarming. After a few moments thought therefore, I simply told the young man that I could not help him. As he was leaving my office he said quite resignedly, but quite good humouredly, that in that case he would have to peddle the drug around various London nightclubs of which he had been given the names and where he had been assured he would find ready buyers.

As soon as he left I picked up the phone and spoke to our solicitor, David Jacobs. His immediate advice was to do nothing, since any contact by 'the Beatles office' with the law on a matter involving drugs could in his view cause unwelcome complications. However, I was unhappy with this advice. On being pressed, David admitted he had high level contacts with the Drugs Squad at Scotland Yard and agreed to speak to them on my behalf. Within the hour I heard from them and two officers shortly appeared in my office. I told them my story. The senior one said he thought they knew who the Vancouver dealers were and asked if I would be prepared to identify the young man if they laid hands on him. I was at first reluctant to agree to this but he said that it would not be necessary to tell the court of my own business connections. I was not sure how this could be, but I agreed.

I heard nothing more of the matter. Clearly, they did not find my visitor. To this day, I do not know whether the Beatles, or Brian Epstein, would have approved of my actions. Probably not.

Not all my visitors presented such problems. Many perfectly serious and respectable people in different areas of show business sought our, or the Beatles', help, financially, artistically, or both. One such was an intense young film producer and director called Peter Watkins, with whom I had a most interesting discussion over lunch. He had produced one successful and highly regarded film for television, an account of the battle of Culloden, and, on the strength of its critical success had subsequently made 'The War Game', a fictionalised (of course) account of the 'next' war and the effects of an atom bomb dropping on London. It was deemed by the television heads to be too horrific and scaring to the populace to be seen. There was too, I think, some pressure from the government to suppress it. I was not sure how Peter Watkins thought we could help him; possibly he felt that the Beatles' endorsement, should they wish to give it, would sway the powers that be. Such was the influence the Beatles had on peoples' minds at the time. Nothing came of our meeting and the film was not seen until a good many years later.

I made it a rule never to interfere in the artistic side of the business. This was for two reasons, equally important: first, I had been invited by Brian Epstein to join his organisation specifically to run the administrative side of the operation. Hence my ridiculously unwieldy formal title of Director and Chief Administrative Executive, which I hardly ever used. And, secondly, I never developed a taste for the product, pop music, and indeed actively disliked much of the output. (When an acquaintance in New York expressed surprise that I could work in pop music without liking it I asked him what was his business.

"Steel manufacturing", he replied. "Do you like steel?" I asked. "Not much", he confessed.) The only time I may have exerted a little influence was when I encouraged Brian Epstein to promote a British tour by the American singers The New Christy Minstrels, one of whose LPs I had enjoyed. They came and were quite a success, financially as well as artistically. But I didn't push my luck by seeking other acts for NEMS to promote.

7
Ticket To Ride

There were a number of changes and additions to the staff of NEMS. Brian Epstein, through the company, bought The Vic Lewis Organisation, a West End booking agency that in addition managed some well-known singers, including Donovan and Matt Monro, as well as the Oscar-winning lyricist Don Black. It also represented in Britain the General Artists Corporation of New York, whose Senior Vice-President, the estimable Norman Weiss, we already knew well, as he arranged all the Beatles' American tours. GAC had on its books many top US singers, including Tony Bennett, Johnny Mathis and The Supremes. The purchase price of the agency was, however, modest. Vic Lewis himself came on to the board of NEMS. He was a middle-aged man who before becoming an agent had been a moderately successful bandleader. While I, who was myself a little older than most of the NEMS people, got on well enough with Vic, his way of doing business and his somewhat self-satisfied personality did not go down well with the existing management and staff. He was clearly pleased at becoming, as he saw it, closely associated with the Beatles, and it was thought that he tried to use promises of appearances by them as a bargaining point in his attempts to attract the biggest American acts to Britain. Bernie Lee could have told him better.

Brian and Vic Lewis never became close. The nadir of their relationship was reached over the debacle of the Beatles' appearances in the Philippines, at the end of the tour which had started in Germany.

Vic Lewis had through his own business contacts arranged for the concerts in Manila. They were successful enough but the Filipino authorities turned against the Beatles over what was perceived, and published, as a snub to the President's wife, Imelda Marcos. She had expected them to attend a lunchtime reception for some two hundred prominent citizens and their children before their two concerts. Neither Brian nor the Beatles had been told of this, and Brian refused to rouse them and bring them to the Presidential Palace when guards came to their hotel to collect them. This was in any case the sort of event which was anathema to the Beatles. The outcome was the withdrawal of any sort of protection and a hair-raising, and genuinely dangerous, escape to the plane leaving Manila airport. Vic Lewis, who was also accompanying the tour, added insult to injury in Brian's eyes by being more concerned over the collection of fees than the Boys' safety. This led to a furious row on the plane between Brian and Vic, which was never really made up.

Another addition to the strength of NEMS Enterprises was Vyvyenne Moynihan, a strong-minded lady with a background in stage and TV presentation. She and Brian had formed a mutual admiration society when she had been employed by a television company and was responsible for negotiating with him for appearances by the Beatles. Although unmarried – she lived with her elderly mother – she evidenced a strong maternal feeling towards Brian, which did not however stop her from frequently pointing out to him what she considered to be his mistakes. "But you can't do that, Brian," she would say to him when he tried to cut through the bureaucracy of TV companies to get what he wanted. He for his part accepted her criticisms meekly enough but continued to do things his way. What Vyvienne seemed not to realise was that Brian, controlling as he did the most sought-after act in the world, could deal with whomever he liked, and was as I have said an innovator in many ways, consciously and unconsciously. In any event, Brian took Vyvyenne onto the staff of NEMS Enterprises' associated company, NEMS

Presentations, which as its name implies was responsible for staging all the shows that NEMS controlled, live and on TV. She worked closely with John Lyndon and they occupied an office of their own in Cork Street, Mayfair. We thus had four offices: Brian's supposedly private suite in Hille House, Stafford Street; the Fan Club in Monmouth Street; the Presentations office in Cork Street; and the main office where I presided in Argyle Street.

To strengthen the accountancy side of NEMS we brought in a qualified accountant, Martin Wesson, a tall, smoothly efficient young man who, as well as overseeing all the royalty and other payments, undertook much of the detailed work in preparing the accounts of the companies in the group, work which had previously been done by our outside accountants.

To my sorrow, Wendy Hanson left, after two years as Brian's Personal Assistant. She had done an excellent job of organising him, as far as was humanly possible and covering for him when, as frequently happened, he was late – often very late – for appointments, or indeed missed them altogether.

Wendy had also established an excellent rapport with the Beatles for whom she performed many services. In an unpublished memoir written before her untimely death in Italy following an accident in her home there in 1991 she wrote:

> "I had met the Beatles in New York the previous year, when I worked for them on their first American tour. We got on extremely well. Their Liverpool accent made me lapse into a bit of Yorkshire, so one day when Paul asked me something I said, quite naturally, 'I don't know love.' (Love was not yet a showbiz expression, but pure north of England.) He gave me a quick look and said 'You're from t'north?' It seemed they had first thought I was American, putting on an English accent. From that moment I was 'OK'. One day during this visit their lawyer called and dictated a brief paragraph to me,

which they all had to sign. Brian wasn't around, so I typed it up, trotted down to their suite, had them sign it and took it back to wait for Brian. He was at first outraged and then impressed. They NEVER signed anything without him there. I didn't find it that extraordinary and pointed out they knew I worked for him, even if only temporarily, but he kept shaking his head in disbelief. I think this was a major factor in his wanting me to work for him.

"Later, in London, as Brian withdrew more into drugs, I became the contact between his office and the boys. It was not just business I was dealing with, but the hiring of their staff and a great deal of personal things, including a lot of shopping. Ringo decided they would like to go to Harrods to Xmas shop. The only way I could envision this was a private visit, so I called their PR lady, who was frightfully grand about it all. She pointed out that the Queen shopped during normal hours and who DID these young men from Liverpool think they were, asking for a private visit. I said fine, I would give her plenty of warning before they came so she could call the police for protection. Silence. I went in to explain the kind of riot that would take place when the fans heard the boys were on the loose in Harrods, and that she would certainly need protection. She suddenly became much nicer and suggested she would think it over and call me back. So one evening, after the shop had officially closed, we all trooped off to Harrods and had the store to ourselves. It was a wonderful fantasy evening. The boys hadn't been able to shop together for so long and they rushed around, especially in the record department (listening to their records and other groups' in the listening booths) and played with all the newest gadgets and toys. They spent a great deal of money (making it worth while for Harrods to keep on the skeleton staff). However, I made a strategic mistake – it was too far away from Xmas and within two weeks of Xmas most of the presents had been given away. This time I asked John Asprey to keep Asprey's open and he was delighted to do so.

"Ringo especially loved Asprey's. Before Maureen's 21st birthday he phoned and asked if I would help him choose a present, he thought a ring. I suggested we go to Cartier's for a change, but he insisted he preferred Asprey's. "It's just like Woolworths, it has so many departments".

"A couple of days before Jane's 21st birthday Paul decided to take her on a surprise trip to Paris. He phoned and prefaced what was to come with 'If you can't do this, say so', to which I was fairly snappy. What he wanted was to charter a private jet to Paris, have a Rolls and English-speaking driver to meet them and then visit boutiques (I substituted the shows at Dior and Yves St. Laurent as in those days there were lots of boutiques in London, but nothing like their shows). Then, dinner at Maxim's with a birthday cake with her name on it. I took care of the transportation and a friend in Paris, Elaine Kennedy, arranged not only for them to go to the collections, but went with them and was able to get the dress that day, so Jane could wear it to dinner that night, which Elaine had arranged at Maxim's. She also took them to her apartment to change. It never occurred to Paul to thank her in any way. A side of his character that always surprised me because his family had meticulous manners, so there seemed to me no excuse for his total self-involvement. When I found out, I sent mountains of roses on his behalf.

"I helped arrange both Ringo's and George's weddings. Again, deep dark secrecy. The night before Ringo was to be married, Don Short of the Daily Mirror kept calling me to confirm a story that was not true. I thought that he suspected the wedding, but in fact he genuinely was checking a lead he had been given on something else. I remember Pattie was absolutely the most beautiful bride in very mod clothes. We always released photos after the event and one paper remarked on a 'very traditional bouquet' (I had bought it at Moyses Stevens!)

"In retrospect it is hard to remember the tremendous news value those four boys had. Also Brian. My own leaving was as small a news story as I could make it, but all the showbiz writers were chasing me around London for days for a statement, as if it was of national importance.

"Life in London ran fairly smoothly as far as my work with the boys was concerned. It was the tours that were a nightmare. America was always immaculately organised by Norman Weiss and his staff. However, it still was a four ring circus on wheels and the best organisation could not always foresee how the fans would find out about exits and car routes. The first year I was with them, leaving for the airport in San Francisco, we were buzzed by kids in battered old convertibles, who had somehow managed to get between the police and our cars, and tried to drive us into the ditch alongside the road. The day before, after the concert at the Cow Palace, where security had been very bad and there had been a lot of injuries, I was driving back to the hotel with Brian and Joan Baez. We were in a large Cadillac and were suddenly stopped by the police who wanted to know who we were. Not safe to go any further they said (by now Brian had his own TV show in the States and was a celebrity in his own right to the kids). The Beatles had only just gotten into the hotel when the cars they were travelling in (brand new Cadillacs) were totally wrecked by the fans jumping all over them. We were transferred to a taxi and driven to the back door of the hotel where two Cadillacs, looking like beaten up toy cars, were pathetically parked outside.

"One year in Chicago Brian decided it was the only place to get a decent meal for days, so the two of us set off between concerts to go to an excellent restaurant. The police said the car was just outside the gate, so out we went. Suddenly we were surrounded by screaming, pushing fans. I couldn't see any sign of the car and began to run. Brian took my arm and said ' Whatever you do, don't run, it will make things worse. Stay calm.' They moved in on us and started pulling Brian's hair and tearing buttons off his coat. Fortunately a police patrol car arrived at that moment and rescued us.

"Another time Brian and I were in a car getting into a stadium. The driver made the mistake of putting down a back window to ask directions and two fans immediately screamed 'It's Brian' and began climbing into the car. Brian made no move, so I did a rather butch imitation of a roadie and put my arm across the window, pushing them back and asking them to get off the car (the danger was one of time, if you stopped for too long they clambered all over it and often turned them on their sides). One little girl promptly bit my finger, and I have the scar to this day. But we got away,

"People wonder why the boys stopped touring. Quite apart from the fact that the kind of music they were making at the end could only be done to their satisfaction in a recording studio, the day to day mechanics were impossibly uncomfortable. No really good hotel would take us (because of the fans hanging around, and then breaking into rooms for souvenirs when we had gone) and from the food point of view alone one ate quite frightful meals. During the day we were usually at baseball stadiums, in the dressing rooms, where the inevitable menu was sent in (usually cold on arrival) over-cooked hamburgers, tired salads and baked potatoes in silver paper. Of course, the concerts themselves were electrifying. The Beatles were totally professional on stage and very much performing artists, and they loved that part. For the rest, they were prisoners of their own security. Endless days in dreary dressing rooms and endless nights and mornings in uniformly dreary hotels.

"Travelling, as I have pointed out, was also risky and rarely smooth. We were arriving in Dallas late one night, having flown that morning from Toronto to somewhere in the South, where they gave two shows. I was sitting with Ringo. I had ordered a drink when we got on the plane and then fallen asleep before I had time to drink it. I missed dinner and woke up as we were landing, spilling the drink all over myself. Ringo was always very gallant and jumped up, organising towels to mop me up. We were landing at a disused army base. Looking down we thought no one was there, but once we had landed about a hundred rather drunk and stoned, teenaged hooligans (they certainly weren't fans) jumped on the plane. They were all over the wings. I was up front with Brian and the boys (we always got off first) so I heard ground control tell the pilot to take off. It wasn't safe as there were not enough police to control the kids. However, he couldn't because by now they were hanging onto the propellers.

"After a very tense twenty minutes, sufficient police finally arrived and the boys and Brian were taken out of the back door on one of those contraptions that usually puts food onto the plane. Bottles were thrown at them, as it raced across the field to waiting cars and one of the roadies had his glasses smashed. When I eventually got to the hotel George was drinking tea. He said 'I'll tell you one thing, if they have a shot at us tomorrow, I'm off home. No showbiz The Show Must Go On for me'.

"Security was a very real worry. On the last tour we had Secret Service bodyguards, which Brian didn't really want the boys to know about in case it worried them. I think they twigged early on and felt rather reassured. One of the funniest drives of my life was from Los Angeles to San Francisco with one of them (an ex-Marine) and Joan Baez. They could not have held more opposite views and I finally had to beg them to talk about anything but not war.

"Although I worked long hours, I did not hang around with Brian and the boys socially. In any case, our tastes were so different and the Beatles, although less than ten years younger than me, seemed a totally different generation. My friends in London were mostly in the classical music world, or friends from Yorkshire.

"One Saturday morning I had to call Brian at home as we worked one Saturday morning a month. I had decided the best way to run a small office was to be democratic so, since there were three girls and me, I took the fourth Saturday in the month when Brian was smashed out of his mind. I hadn't told anyone about his drugs. I spoke to Brian as one would to a rather naughty child (I didn't realise I did this under those circumstances until his chauffeur pointed it out, much later).

"After 'Help!' the Beatles owed United Artists one more film. Al Brodax, of King Features in New York (the company that made a Beatles cartoon series for US TV) had come up with an idea of an animated feature film, using their music. While we were in New York, he came to see Brian on a very bad day. Brian was very 'high' and very irritable and so rude to Al, whom I had never met before, that my heart went out to him. Some months later Al had a script he wanted Brian to see of 'The Yellow Submarine'. Brian insisted that Al personally bring it to London. Al demurred, as it was his children's half term from school. Brian insisted he come, saying however that he would see him on the Friday morning so he could leave for the airport by noon.

"The day before the appointment Al had the good sense to call from New York and, after checking with Brian, the appointment was confirmed. Unfortunately, it was one of Brian's worst periods. He had almost stopped coming into the office and would sleep all day and gamble and whatever at night. My secretary, Joanne, had gone to be his secretary and worked out of his house, where he now did nearly all his work.

"Al came for his appointment, and then the next day, and then the next. Ten days went by and he had not seen Brian (nor had I). Finally, one Friday evening he came into my office and announced he would wait until Brian came in to sign his mail. There was no mail to sign! To divert him I invited him to have a drink with me at an hotel round

the corner. As we were leaving Brian called and demanded to talk to me (I was trying to avoid this in front of Al). How could I, he wanted to know, keep someone as important as Al waiting for ten days, why hadn't he been told Al was in London? It was total nonsense time. He knew perfectly well about Al's waiting around for him but he was stoned out of his mind. I was so angry, I gave in my notice on the spot.

"Giving in notice had become something of a ritual, I must admit. One Saturday morning, I was doing my turn and Brian had sworn he would be in by ten. I had to speak to him as we were giving a rather large dinner for Cilla the next night, Sunday, and the venue had to be decided. This was the kind of detail Brian still liked to decide himself, so I phoned the house (for the umpteenth time) asking to speak to him. Finally he came to the phone and told me to wait for him, he'd be in 'sometime' during the afternoon. I pointed out that I'd been there all morning, that it was almost one o'clock and I had a lunch date, after which I had to go shopping (the London shopping hours were difficult enough on Saturday afternoons and non-existent on Sundays). He was furious and raged that he paid me more than anyone else on his personal staff and if he wanted me 48 hours a day, then I'd better be there 48 hours a day. By the time Brian came into the office, my letter of resignation was on the desk.

"But the Beatles always persuaded me to stay, saying they had only just got used to me and that I was the only one who seemed able to handle Brian.

"The Al Brodax time, I really meant to make it stick but the boys cannily got me alone at the beginning of a press conference (sending everyone else out of the room, even Neil and Mal) and offering to send me on a holiday anywhere I wanted to go.

"I decided on a six week leave of absence, unpaid (Yorkshire independence to the end), and off I went. But not quite. Before I left I discovered that Brian was lunching at Les Ambassadeurs, a very chic London club whose owners I fortunately knew, so I arranged for Al Brodax to have a table there too and he just 'happened' to be there when Brian was, and got the go ahead for his script.

"Finally, working with Brian became so impossible that I really and truly resigned."

Wendy told me of another American tour experience. She had found herself shivering at an outdoor concert in San Francisco. One of the entourage took pity on her and gave her a leather bomber jacket to wear. The Beatles were entranced by the sight of the ever-elegant Wendy in this garment and, surrounding her, autographed the jacket, as did the two road managers, Neil Aspinall and Mal Evans, along with several others on the tour. When she got back to the hotel, the chambermaid cleaning Wendy's room admired the autographed bomber jacket so extravagantly that Wendy on an impulse gave it to her. When she told me this later she pointed out that it was not her type of garment and that she would probably never have worn it again. It was only some years later, when Sotheby's and Christie's started selling Beatles' memorabilia for huge sums, that she realised what her act of generosity had probably cost her. "It could have been my pension!" she mourned.

Brian, despite his difficult ways with Wendy as her employer, was very fond of her and from time to time took pleasure in taking her out. At Christmas 1965, the Beatles had no Christmas show so Brian celebrated by taking Wendy and myself to Covent Garden for a performance of the ballet 'Cinderella', adorned by Robert Helpmann's and Frederick Ashton's ugly sisters. "The office Christmas outing", Wendy and I said. Notwithstanding such happy occasions, Brian's professional treatment of her eventually, as she wrote, became too much. She left, after threatening several times to do so.

Sometime later, she came back temporarily, to do a specific job. The Beatles wanted the cover of the 'Sergeant Pepper's Lonely Hearts Club Band' LP to include photographs of very many well-known people surrounding them, in fact as it was eventually issued. EMI Records insisted on having the approval of all the celebrities concerned before they would release the record with the desired cover. Brian realised that the best person to get the necessary clearances was Wendy, first, because she was more likely than most to know, or to find out, how to contact the people or their representatives; secondly, because she could be very persuasive; and, thirdly, because she was efficient and would get the job done quickly. He therefore got in touch with her, agreed a fee and set her down with an office and a phone. She spent the next few days, and nights, tracking down the likes of Johnny Weissmuller, Marlon Brando and Marlene Dietrich or their representatives, and finally got all the needed clearances. (This was not quite the end of the story. The Board of Directors of EMI considered the record sleeve and Lord Shawcross, eminent lawyer, former Attorney General, stated firmly that the photograph of Mahatma Gandhi could not possibly be included, as this would cause great offence in India and to Indians worldwide. A palm tree was therefore hastily drawn in to cover the offending likeness, which fortunately was at one end of the front row.)

After a successful period in London as a public relations advisor to several prominent classical musicians, Wendy went back to New York to head the press office at the Metropolitan Opera. Later on, before going to live permanently in the house she had bought and restored in Tuscany, she advised numerous American musicians, including the conductor Lorin Maazel. She had an enormous range of friends, and I was constantly surprised at who might come up and gossip when she and I were dining out in London. She had many contacts in the film world as well as that of music: Rod Steiger was a particular friend whom I met several times with her, as was the Italian director Luchino Visconti. She was always a joy to be with and I miss her. As do many.

A man called Peter Brown came to work for NEMS in London, initially without any specific job. A friend of Brian's from Liverpool, he came originally from a suburb of Birkenhead, the run-down shipbuilding town across the river Mersey from Liverpool. He became friendly with Brian when he was working in the record department of Lewis's, a large department store, and later went to work at the NEMS shops. I first met him, with Brian, during one of my trips home while I was still working in America. After Brian left Liverpool, Brown took over the record department at the main NEMS store. The shops were then largely controlled by Brian's younger brother, Clive. One day Brian told me with some embarrassment of a conversation he had had with Clive, who had told him he was going to dispense with Brown's services. Clive had asked if there was any opening for him in the NEMS Enterprises operation in London. Brian agreed to take him on, not least since, as I knew, he liked having his friends about him. He made himself useful in a number of ways and was helpful to Brian personally during the latter's increasingly frequent depressions and bouts of drug taking. After Wendy Hanson left, Peter Brown took on the job of Brian's personal assistant. Many people commented on how he modelled himself on Brian, to the extent that their voices on the telephone became indistinguishable except to those who knew Brian well. He eventually moved in with Brian at his Belgravia house and helped in many ways, including, according to a TV interview he gave some years later, helping him to get marijuana. He could perhaps have been too helpful at times and Brian's chauffeur, Bryan Barrett, relates in a book published in 2000 how Brian asked him if he would kill Peter Brown, and what would it cost. Needless to say, nothing came of this.

Some junior staff came and went at NEMS, although the core of the original group from Liverpool, exemplified by Laurie on the switchboard, remained.

Brian Epstein, for his part, had always wanted to be someone in his own right, rather than just the manager of the Beatles and other successful pop artists. He had relished the opportunities which came his way to make personal appearances on radio and television: he had been a radio 'castaway' on Desert Island Discs (on which he nominated as his favourite record the Beatles' latest single record, 'She's a Woman', which was duly played: a useful plug to the BBC radio audience) and had appeared on television more than once as a panellist on Juke Box Jury. He had also made one or two appearances on American TV introducing pop acts, which had not however attracted much attention. And then there was the Saville Theatre venture. Although presenting some of his favourite artists there, such as the Four Tops, Chuck Berry and Little Richard, and acting as impresario to some of the stage shows mounted there gave him personal satisfaction, the venture, of which more later, was not a commercial success. He was particularly pleased when asked in 1966 to present at the New Arts Theatre Club a play by fellow Liverpudlian Alan Plater, 'Smashing Day'. Although the theatre is very small, it carries prestige and the club has a serious membership.

The play was produced by John Fernald, a former director of the Liverpool Playhouse repertory theatre and subsequently of the Royal Academy of Dramatic Art when Brian himself studied there. The star of the play was Hywel Bennett, then largely unknown but later on to become a well-known face in TV sitcoms as well as in more serious productions. (Another performer was the then unknown Ben Kingsley, who later became world famous in the title role of Richard Attenborough's film 'Gandhi'. He is now Sir Ben.) When rehearsals were well advanced John Fernald fell ill and he suggested that Brian should take over the stage direction right up to its opening to the

BRIAN EPSTEIN IN HIS SUITE AT THE WALDORF TOWERS, NEW YORK IN 1966

club audience. Though somewhat daunted, Brian undertook this with enthusiasm. We all realised that, although this was far from a gimmick, the publicity resulting from having the Beatles' manager direct a serious play could only help the production. I watched him rehearsing the caste several times and, knowing him as well as I did, was impressed by the seriousness and dedication with which he went about it. In refreshment intervals he would go off into a corner by himself with the script, his notes and a sandwich and prepare for the next period, rather than, as he would normally have done, join a group for a convivial lunch or a few drinks.

The play had mixed reviews. Some were in fact quite respectable. But Brian was disappointed that 'Smashing Day' was not a smashing success and had only a brief run. He didn't seem able to do anything to prove his own artistic quality.

In sum, Brian suffered a disappointing time, and there was always the knowledge that the Beatles' management contract would expire in late 1967 to haunt him. In view of their increasingly independent ways, it seemed likely that they would not wish to renew their agreement with NEMS on the same terms; but, had Brian lived, there is no doubt that there would have continued to be an association between him and the boys, though probably looser and less lucrative to NEMS, and hence to Brian.

Brian's worries led him to increasingly self-indulgent behaviour. He became largely dependent on a variety of pills and, as Wendy Hanson related, seldom appeared in his office or kept regular hours. He took up with a number of unsavoury characters. One of these was a young American he met on one of his trips to the USA. His name was John Gillespie, nicknamed Dizz. Brian was warned by his friend Nat Weiss, among others, that Dizz was nothing more than a common or garden hustler but Brian was infatuated with him and brought him to London. Dizz persuaded him that he had some singing or other artistic talent and so, to regularise his stay in England, Brian agreed to put him under contract to NEMS Enterprises. Accordingly, he asked me to draw up a contract for a management agreement between the company and Dizz. I remonstrated, since the young man had displayed no talent at all, except for sponging off Brian, but he was adamant. The contract provided for an advance against putative earnings of something like £50 per week. This sum was however far from enough to satisfy Dizz, who helped himself to increasingly large amounts of cash and valuables from Brian. He was a thief as well as a hustler. Eventually, Brian did lose patience and sent him back to America.

However, Dizz surfaced again when Brian was in Los Angeles a short time later, and persuaded him that he had turned over a new leaf. He proceeded to steal Brian's briefcase (and Nat Weiss's as well); it contained a large amount of cash, Beatles' American tour contracts and a bottle of pills. Weiss had Dizz entrapped and arrested, Brian's briefcase was recovered, minus the pills and much of the money but with the contracts intact. The affair left Brian saddened, though unfortunately no wiser, and he continued to form incautious liaisons. One day when Bob Casper, Walter Hofer's young partner, was in London, I took him to see Brian at the house in Chapel Street to discuss some business matters, since Brian showed no sign of coming to his office for this or any other purpose. Bob Casper and I left our taxi round the corner in Belgrave Square and walked the short distance to the house. It was mid-afternoon and as we approached we saw some sort of scuffle going on at the doorstep. Brian's chauffeur, a loyal and burly ex-serviceman, was in the process of ejecting quite forcefully a young man who clearly had not intended to leave when Brian asked him to. Bob Casper and I had our meeting with Brian who appeared unembarrassed by the incident. Bob was too tactful to refer to it during the meeting, and indeed it was never mentioned between us.

It was clear even to Brian that something had to be done to clear up his life and his career as a manager, or entrepreneur, or whatever else he intended to become. At this time, in1966/67, he was still in his early thirties, but even now, despite the fame and fortune that were already his, he was unhappy and unfulfilled. A good many years previously, when we were both still living in Liverpool, he had told me, almost boastfully, that a psychiatrist to whom his parents had referred him had pronounced him to be of a psychopathic nature; happily, this condition, if the diagnosis was correct, had never manifested itself in the acts of violence often associated with it. Brian remained a kind man, wanting to be loved but unable to find the person or persons who could give him the affection he needed; unfortunately, his sexual tastes militated against his discovering happiness of this sort. Around this time he made what was perceived as a suicide attempt by means of a drug overdose, leading to psychiatric hospital treatment.

He was determined to try to relax some more. With this end in mind he bought a house in the country. It was not a large place, but was an attractive brick-built house of some antiquity, buried deep in the Sussex countryside about fifty miles south of London. It stood in hilly country and was quite remote, even from the nearest village. Brian made it even more secluded by having the wall separating the garden from the lane leading to it heightened, so that both house and garden became invisible from the road. Very soon after this purchase Brian invited me down to see it, and I was delighted to find him happy and relaxed in these new surroundings. He proudly showed me round the house and grounds, and during the weekend we went to Brighton, where he bought numerous items from antique shops, including a canteen of silver-plate cutlery. He had already installed in the house a mixture of new and old furniture, explaining that this was to be a complete contrast to the formality of his Belgravia house, which had been fashionably decorated by Kenneth Partridge. He had also found a married couple to act as cook/housekeeper and gardener, who were installed in a flat in the outbuildings. All in all, this seemed an excellent move and Brian was insistent that, although he would entertain friends in the country, the house was entirely for relaxation and that he would spend as much time there as he could, away from the pressures of his business and social life in London.

8
It's All Too Much

The accounts side of the business was one which I did not, it seemed, have to worry much about. The team of Martin Wesson, Monty and a couple of assistants handled incoming and outgoing payments with considerable efficiency, and queries from the artists were very few. Bryce Hanmer Isherwood looked after audits and taxation matters, and Jim Isherwood was always available to give any needed advice.

Then, suddenly, a crisis arose. Jim Isherwood had personal problems of which we had not been aware and left the country without warning accompanied by a lady who was not his wife. One of his partners, Harry Pinsker, once Jim had been located somewhere in the Caribbean, flew out to see him, and as a result of their discussions Jim resigned from the partnership, which forthwith became 'Bryce Hanmer', dropping Jim's name. Brian Epstein and I were shocked, as Jim knew more about the financial affairs of the Beatles and NEMS than anyone, and we would miss his presence and advice. Moreover, Brian, ever sensitive to any occurrence that might adversely affect the Beatles, was concerned that there might be some connection between their finances and Jim's disappearance. We therefore contacted the leading accountancy firm of Peat Marwick Mitchell and asked them to conduct an immediate examination into the books and records of the company and the artists.

While this was going on Harry Pinsker, whom I had barely met before, came to see me to discuss the matter and to request that his firm, now minus Jim Isherwood, continue to handle our business. It was a somewhat embarrassing meeting as at that time I could give him no such assurance, although I had no doubt of his personal integrity and of the firm's efficiency.

However, Peat Marwick Mitchell concluded their work very swiftly and Brian and I were invited to learn the outcome by the supervising partner, Mr (later Sir) John Grenside, who later became the head of the firm. He was able to assure us that all was well with the accounts and that there was no reason to believe that Jim Isherwood's departure had anything to do with them. Greatly relieved, Brian, impressed by the firm's efficiency, suggested that they might like to take over from Bryce Hanmer. Mr Grenside, courteously and fairly tactfully, indicated that pop music was not the sort of business in which they cared to be interested, and declined the honour. Surprised, we left, and I was able to tell Harry Pinsker that his firm could continue to act for the Beatles and NEMS.

Mr Grenside's response continued to surprise me, although I later learned that at about the same time the Rolling Stones had been turned down by a leading merchant bank. Within a few years accountancy firms, merchant banks and consultants were falling over themselves offering their services to pop groups who, like the Beatles and the Rolling Stones, were generating huge amounts of money and were a lucrative source of income for tax advisers and professionals of all types.

Another consequence of Jim Isherwood's departure from the scene concerned Northern Songs. He was prevailed upon without difficulty to resign his directorship since he had no longer any connection with Lennon and McCartney and their music. Brian Epstein, with the agreement of John and Paul, thereupon asked me, likewise with Dick James's and Charles Silver's approval, to join the board, representing, with Brian, the interests of NEMS and the songwriters. Although I had frequently acted as Brian's substitute at meetings of the directors, both formal and informal, I was gratified to be confirmed as a director in my own right of this public company. The appointment did nonetheless lead to some trouble ahead.

A major problem, which had been bubbling for sometime, came to the boil soon after: merchandising.

It is perhaps a measure of the innocence of the times, and perhaps even of those of us involved, that no one realised the potential of the Beatles as a merchandising commodity until the marketing of the group had grown so large and cumbersome that it was spinning out of control.

Nowadays, of course, income from merchandising comes a close second to income from record or ticket sales. Major artists such as Michael Jackson sign multi-million dollar deals to promote soft drinks, and many tours by bands like the Rolling Stones are so expensive to stage that they would not happen without the support of the companies willing to underwrite a tour in return for the exposure – and implied recommendation – their products will receive.

Prior to the Beatles, merchandising was a gimmick, a novelty, something – usually little more than a programme, poster or badge – produced so that the fans would have a keepsake or memento of a concert or public appearance. They were manufactured on a break-even basis, to increase a band's public profile. Often they were produced by fan clubs as gifts or special offers for members. In an age that now seems shockingly ignorant of marketing techniques, they were regarded as a minor factor in a publicity campaign, and certainly nothing to do with the art and business of making and selling records. By 1963 it had become apparent that the Beatles presented a merchandising phenomenon that no-one – the band, their management, the merchandising companies or even the fans – could fully comprehend. Such was the fever for the group that fans would have bought virtually anything that had the band's name on it. When the group first became famous, many manufacturers of toys and novelties realised that there was potential in associating their wares with the Beatles. Most notable in the plethora of Beatles-related knick-knacks was the Beatles wig. In the early 1960s their collar-length hair was fashionably 'long', or at least it seemed so in the days before the hippy trend for long, flowing locks and was virtually the Beatles' trademark. No matter that these hairpieces were evidently false, their association with the Beatles made them an essential purchase for thousands of fans.

As it became apparent that the Beatles represented a hitherto unheard-of potential in merchandising, many other manufacturers of pop ephemera wanted to cash in on their popularity. This was particularly acute in America where manufacturers were already producing a boggling array of trivia – pens, posters badges, tee-shirts and innumerable other items, some with the slenderest link to the Beatles – for a market with an insatiable appetite for anything with 'The Beatles' inscribed on it.

In 1963 neither Brian Epstein nor anyone working for him knew anything of merchandising. In fairness, it has to be said that this was the case with most artists and managers at the time. Brian's time was consumed with the artistic career of the Beatles and he had little time for the boring minutiae of business meetings and contracts. When wig-makers and other manufacturers approached him wanting to acquire the rights to produce some other new Beatles-related gimmick, Brian simply referred them to his solicitors, M.A. Jacobs and Son. David Jacobs, the senior partner in the firm, which specialised in entertainers and entertainment law, also had little inkling of just how important pop merchandising would become and delegated the work to a member of his staff. It is quite easy in hindsight to see that the merchandising was mishandled simply out of naiveté, but before anybody knew it matters were getting out of hand.

Because no-one was keeping an adequate check on just what was happening with the Beatles' merchandising a number of deals were struck which, although bringing in a share of income to the Beatles via NEMS, were not as advantageous as they could have been. But before anyone realised this the situation was already fraught with acrimony, accusations and lawsuits.

Sometime before my arrival a group of young entrepreneurs, headed by a man called Nicky Byrne, offered to handle the whole business of merchandising the Beatles. The offer was appealing: it would immediately take the onus off Brian Epstein and would, at the same time, ensure an income from the efforts of Byrne and his colleagues. They formed a company called Stramsact (said to be an anagram, somewhat laboured though not inappropriate, of Smart Acts). It is hard to imagine it happening now, but the deal was nego-tiated through the offices of M.A. Jacobs and Son. NEMS would receive for the Beatles what now seems a derisory ten per cent of the income generated. Brian soon realised that this percentage was ludicrously inadequate and in the summer of 1964 it was increased to 46 per cent. Even this, subject to NEMS's 25 per cent manage-ment commission, meant that the Beatles themselves shared a mere 34.5 percent (just over 8½ per cent each) of the phenomenal sales being generated. Stramsact Ltd set up an American subsidiary which they called Seltaeb (try spelling it backwards) Inc to handle the vast American market. Seltaeb's president was Nicky Byrne. He was one of half a dozen partners in the venture, of whom one was the Earl of St. Germans's heir, Lord Eliot, and another was Malcolm Evans, not to be confused with the Beatles' road manager of the same name. After all the trouble blew up, related below, we heard of discord in their ranks, with one or more of them allegedly suing another or others.

When I joined NEMS at the end of 1964 there were already rumblings of discontent among manufacturers who were unhappy about merchandising rights they had been granted. A typical, though hypothetical, instance of the confusion that bedevilled the Beatles merchandising deals would be a case where, say, the London solicitors had granted the exclusive right to make and sell Beatles watches in Britain to a UK manufacturer while, later on, Seltaeb purported to grant a worldwide licence for 'jewellery' bearing the Beatles' names and likenesses to an American manufacturer. The latter might well consider that the licence included the right to sell Beatles watches. Thus each manufacturer believed they had an exclusive licence covering watches. There were a number of such instances, as there were threats of writs involving NEMS and the Beatles.

There were also mounting suspicions that accounts produced by Stramsact/Seltaeb were defective, as well as late. When challenged, Stramsact/Seltaeb countered that they were hampered by existing licences of the sort mentioned above. They also claimed they had not been given full details of existing grants of rights when they took over the merchandising. They, like NEMS, were being threatened with legal actions by disgruntled licensees. Unquestionably, there were faults on both sides, although matters were not made any easier by allegations that Nicky Byrne in New York was living the high-life off the proceeds of Beatles licensing with, it was reported, a twenty-four hour limousine service and a lavish lifestyle to match. This made Brian Epstein furious, and eventually he demanded that something be done to control the licensing and curb the excesses.

Accordingly, after I was installed at NEMS, we instructed Walter Hofer in New York to launch proceedings against Seltaeb, in which Stramsact in England inevitably became involved. Full, up-to-date accounts were demanded, together with payment of sums past due, together with interest and damages. In the usual way of American litigation, the amounts swiftly escalated to what seemed to me fairly ludicrous amounts. Stramsact/Seltaeb swiftly counter-attacked by suing NEMS and the Beatles for substantial damages arising, it was claimed, from conflicting licenses, leading to loss of income, damage to business and so on. One swift and inevitable result of this litigation was that manufacturers who had been considering applying for licenses for their own proposed Beatles products took fright and decided not to go ahead, for fear of becoming involved in the legal tangle. The Beatles thus lost a considerable amount of potential income.

For all his business and negotiating skills, Walter Hofer was not experienced in litigation and his reports to me of the progress of the proceedings in the New York courts were not particularly encouraging, although he continued to assure me that all would be well in the long run. However, a crisis arose when at one stage of the court proceedings the judge demanded that Brian Epstein appear in person. (Even the judge realised that it would be pointless to summon the Beatles to appear; this would, if it ever happened, be counter-productive to Seltaeb's case, since the boys were so popular that their personal involvement would have produced widespread sympathy for their cause – as well as a riot outside the courthouse.) Brian simply refused to go to New York to get involved in the litigation, instead adopting the stance of an ostrich burying its head in the sand. In any case, Walter assured us that he could get round the judge's requirement. He was wrong and we lost that round of the proceedings, with damages of $5,000,000 being awarded against NEMS. Walter continued to exude confidence that we would win on the appeal which he immediately launched, but it was apparent that we were in serious trouble.

Following a series of transatlantic phone calls between Brian, Walter and myself, Brian at last realised that things were going badly wrong and that he – and, worse, the Beatles – could be made liable for huge amounts of damages. Moreover, they would suffer from the adverse publicity of losing the case. He therefore spoke to his New York attorney friend, Nat Weiss, and asked him to look into the matter. Weiss did so and swiftly advised us to seek help from litigation experts who could render us more assistance than Walter Hofer, by now out of his depth, could provide. Brian agreed and an appointment was made with Louis Nizer, a senior partner in the prominent New York law firm of Phillips, Nizer, Benjamin, Krim and Ballon. Louis Nizer was probably the best known American trial lawyer of his day, having acted, mostly successfully, for a string of high-profile clients, and his examinations in court were legendary in America.

Brian, David Jacobs and I set off for New York together and on arrival conferred with Nat Weiss. The next day, the four of us went to our meeting with Louis Nizer in his office. Walter Hofer was not invited to accompany us; though piqued at being replaced, I am sure that he was relieved at being eased out of this particular situation. In fact, the debacle did nothing to harm our working relationship with Walter and he continued to act for NEMS and the Beatles on general matters.

The meeting with Louis Nizer was an experience in itself. His firm had offices in the old Paramount building in Times Square, a rather unusual base for an important law firm, although this was probably explained by the fact that they had long acted for many companies and personalities prominent in the film and entertainment industry. Mr Nizer's own office, high up in the building, was enormous, with stained glass windows that gave it a cathedral-like atmosphere. He was quite a small man and his desk was positioned on a small dais. Clients had to look up at him from their chairs below the dais. This slight artificiality was unnecessary since his personality made him the focus of any meeting, and I realised after our meeting how he could dominate a courtroom. One of my regrets from this whole episode is that I never saw Nizer in action in a courtroom.

Needless to say, he agreed to take on the case, and was obviously pleased to be consulted on behalf of the Beatles. He had had a brief opportunity to apprise himself of the status of the litigation and assured us that his and his firm's best efforts would ensure that the $5 million judgment, passed on technical grounds because of Brian Epstein's refusal to appear, was set aside. The firm would secure a delay in the proceedings during the substitution of Phillips, Nizer, Benjamin, Krim and Ballon for Walter's firm. At this first meeting, Brian asked most particularly that Mr Nizer should himself appear for us at the main trial of the action, if it came to that. Mr Nizer was, I recall, a little evasive in his answer: a commercial lawsuit such as this was not really his forte: dramatic appeals to the jury on behalf of alleged murderers or wronged film stars were more his style. However, he assured us of his close attention to our interests.

When we returned from our meeting direct to the Plaza Hotel, Brian and I each found in our respective rooms books written by Louis Nizer and personally inscribed by him. Brian received his autobiography, 'My Life In Court', while I got his 'An Analysis and Commentary on the Official Warren Commission Report', the famous commission that investigated the Kennedy assassination. Louis Nizer was clearly an expert at client relations, and these tomes convinced us we had a powerful ally in the coming legal battle.

The partner assigned to our case was an excellent lawyer, an Englishman by birth, Simon Rose. He was, he told me, originally from Yorkshire where he had qualified and practised as a solicitor. He had emigrated to the USA some years earlier and had passed the bar examination in New York State, where he now practised in Phillips, Nizer as a trial lawyer. He retained, however, a total Englishness in appearance, accent and manner. He even affected a bowler hat and furled umbrella with his impeccably tailored suits, and it was a remarkable sight to see him striding through Times Square, which at this time was full of tourists, beggars and hustlers of all descriptions, to the offices in the Paramount building. There was nothing at all affected about his work and methods, however, and he set about familiarising himself with the complexities of our litigation with immense thoroughness, coming to London a few weeks later to study the background and documentation further, and to confer with M.A. Jacobs and Son.

The time came for pre-trial examinations of, among others, Brian Epstein and myself. These were formal examinations on oath; they are normally held in the offices of one of the law firms acting in the case in question, with a stenographer present to record every word. By this time, however, Simon Rose and the principal opposing counsel – for Seltaeb – Jerome Katz, were at daggers drawn and the examinations had to be held on neutral ground, in a private room at the New York State Courthouse in downtown Manhattan with a referee, a retired judge, present to see fair play. Once again, Brian and I flew to New York, and the next day Brian was sworn in and interrogated. It was an exceedingly unpleasant experience for him, as he had to admit that he knew virtually nothing of the numerous contractual arrangements, in Britain or America, which were the basis of the dispute. He also had to admit that his knowledge of the accounts and financial affairs of the merchandising was sketchy, to say the least. He had, of course, always concentrated on the artistic careers of the Beatles, their tours, their TV and film appearances, their song-writing and recording. Here, he was subject to such questioning, all on the record, as "Do you mean to say, Mr Epstein, that you had no knowledge of such-and-such a contract, which could earn your clients, the Beatles, hundreds of thousands of dollars?" I tried in breaks during questioning, which went on for several days, to assure Brian that I would secure the answers to all counsel's questions by the time my own turn came a week or two later, but this was little comfort to him. Fortunately, these hearings were private, so there was no reporting access for the press; but Brian's experience made us determined that the case should not come to trial, and we urged Simon Rose to do everything possible to bring it to such a state that it would be settled on reasonable terms and with the least possible damage to the Beatles.

When my own turn for pre-trial examination came I managed to survive the one day it took relatively unscathed, but my inevitable discomfort was not eased by the fact that it took place during a transit strike in New York. The limousine which transported Simon Rose, an assistant and myself from Midtown Manhattan to the courthouse was delayed by abnormally heavy traffic, and on our return uptown in the afternoon progress was so slow that at one point I was able to get out of the car, queue at a restaurant for coffee and cakes for the party, including the driver, and return ten minutes later to find that the limousine had barely moved. An uncomfortable experience all round, and drinks and dinner that evening were even more welcome than usual.

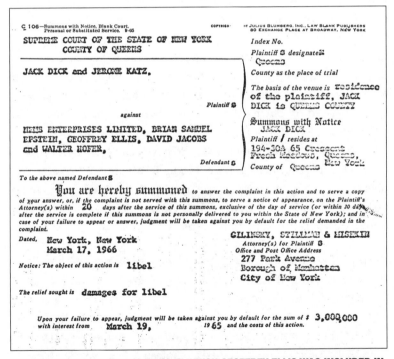

A COPY OF THE WRIT REFERRED TO IN WHICH GEOFFREY ELLIS WAS INCLUDED IN AN ACTION FOR $3,000,000. THIS ACTION FORTUNATELY CAME TO NOTHING

Following the pre-trial examinations, tempers on both sides did not lighten and there were further acrimonious exchanges. To my dismay, I was personally named in one of several fresh writs issued by Seltaeb's lawyers. This was for libel, resulting from written instructions we had issued sometime earlier to Walter Hofer in which allegedly defamatory comments had been made about the lawyers in question. Brian Epstein, David Jacobs, Walter Hofer and myself were named, along with NEMS Enterprises Limited, in the writ in which damages of $3 million were claimed. This was pure harassment, of course, but if this particular action had been successful I was far from sure where my share of the damages would have come from.

It was a tribute to Simon Rose and his efforts that all the proceedings were eventually settled. Accountings were made, damages assessed on both sides and a balance was struck. By then, claims had mounted to a sum approaching $100 million, but the balancing out resulted in our paying to Seltaeb Inc. less than £100,000, a sum which would barely cover their costs. As for the costs on our side, Brian insisted on paying them out of his own pocket since he felt personally responsible for the mess. There is no doubt that the Beatles lost out on the huge amounts that could have been earned by properly controlled merchandising. There is equally no doubt that Brian was deeply scarred by the experience and that this helped to lead to the depression and dependence on drugs which were coming to dominate his private life at this time.

Despite the almost total collapse of any Beatles' merchandising strategy resulting from the Seltaeb case, there were still occasional business propositions put to us in America. One was by a famous soft drinks company, which proposed to 'give' the Beatles one of their bottling plants in New Jersey and at the same time pay them $1 million. At first sight it seemed a painless way to earn such a sum, even though clearly the point of the deal would be the public association between the company and the Beatles. When we expressed a guarded interest and asked for full details it was made clear that the company expected a full product endorsement by the Beatles on every possible occasion, particularly at public performances. They would also be required to make regular, highly publicised visits to 'their' bottling plant. It was not hard to turn this offer down.

Events were in any case to thwart any serious attempts to realise the potential of the Beatles as a merchandising phenomenon. By the time the Seltaeb/Stramsact situation was finally sorted out two factors would militate against this. For one, Brian was still bruised by his experience in the American legal system and, if anything, was even less keen to involve himself in merchandising, something he still considered peripheral to the essence of the Beatles, namely their music. The Beatles themselves were also changing. Although their fan base remained huge they were moving away from the commercialism that might have lent itself to merchandising. As the hair grew longer and the clothes wilder the Beatles – with the notable exception of George – were increasingly uninterested in money.

On the other hand, Brian did not let the merchandising debacle deter him from starting up a business in America in partnership with his lawyer friend, Nat Weiss. They called their company Nemperor Holdings. 'Nemperor' was the telegraphic address of NEMS Enterprises in London and Brian felt it was an appropriate name for his American venture. Initially, the company had some success in managing a group called The Cyrkle, one of whose single records, 'Red Rubber Ball', reached the number two spot in the US charts. But this proved just a flash in the pan and the company did not prosper. It might have done had Brian survived.

A matter which occupied much of my own time at this period concerned the production of the film 'Yellow Submarine', mentioned by Wendy Hanson in her memoir. A series of half-hour animated cartoons of the Beatles had been produced, by agreement, by an

American production company, King Features, a subsidiary of the Hearst Corporation, the media conglomerate. These children's programmes had had successful runs on television, initially in the USA and Britain, where they were shown on Saturday mornings. The individual producer for King Features was Al Brodax, whose ambition was to produce a full-length animated feature film of the Beatles for theatrical release. At the time, the Beatles 'owed' United Artists a third film, following "A Hard Day's Night" and "Help!", since Brian Epstein had agreed a three picture deal following the success of the first film. The trouble was that the boys were becoming increasingly disenchanted with their work in public as the Beatles; all they wanted to do was to make their music and the only way they could do that to their satisfaction was by recording. In the studio, with only George Martin as an equal to guide them, they found it uniquely possible to develop their joint artistic career as musicians. They were therefore disinclined to waste their time, as they saw it, making another fairly idiotic film. Brian tried to interest them in various film projects including scripts by, among others, Joe Orton and Alun Owen, but he too was half-hearted in his efforts, realising that if he was to retain his management hold over them he must to a large extent fall in with their own desires.

On the face of it the cartoon film would be a way out of the impasse. The Beatles would have no personal involvement other than a requirement to supply three original, previously unrecorded songs, and with some persuasion United Artists agreed to accept distribution of the cartoon film as fulfilment of the three-picture contract. Al Brodax therefore rolled into action. The difficulty that then presented itself was that there was no chemistry, to put it politely, between Brian and himself. Al was very informal, slapping Brian on the back; Brian was generally formal in business meetings. Indeed, some found him arrogant. As Wendy Hanson recorded, Brian did everything possible to avoid a meeting with him, and when they did meet Al found Brian impossible to deal with. He recalled to me one meeting in New York, when he was attempting to secure Brian's signature to the agreement for distribution worldwide by United Artists, Brian had objected, saying "Britain is mine!" Al cited this assertion as being typical of Brian's arrogance in his dealings with him. I, as so often happened, was thrust into the role of go-between and mediator. Fortunately, I found Al entirely likeable: an honest hustler in his own interests, he would take every opportunity to get his own way and would use his native New Yorker's charm to achieve his ends. He was very informal in appearance at all times and once, when taking me with his wife Joan to a promised celebratory dinner at the Connaught in London, was turned away from the restaurant as he was not wearing a tie. Since, as he was wearing a polo-necked sweater, he could not put one on, we had to go elsewhere.

The actual physical production took place in London and I had the chance to observe the amazingly detailed work that goes into the making of an animated film, with every single frame being completed individually. There were problems over the story-line: long after the song 'Yellow Submarine', sung on the original recording by Ringo, had been selected as the basis of the feature, script difficulties arose and Al Brodax brought in Eric Segal to doctor it. He was the bright young Harvard professor who later wrote the novel 'Love Story' and the script for the immensely popular film based on it, as well as other successful novels and films. He was a delightful person but was given little time by Al to socialise during his stint in London. I heard him relate in a BBC radio programme many years later how much he had disliked the work, as every aspect of the storyline had to be cleared, through unsympathetic intermediaries, with all four Beatles and Brian Epstein. He also claimed that Al Brodax had not allowed him to attend Brian Epstein's funeral, as the day it took place provided an opportunity for him, Eric Segal, to work uninterruptedly, everyone else concerned being absent from their offices and in many cases out of London.

Moreover, there were delays in the supply by the Beatles of their three new songs, which naturally had to be fitted into the story; this could of course be done only after they had been received. All in all, Al had a hard time, not eased by Brian's continuing uncooperativeness. Quite early one morning Brian, after a particularly acrimonious telephone conversation with Al, asked me to go and tell him that the deal was off and that there would be no further co-operation at all. The production was at a fairly advanced stage but I duly went to see Al, then staying at the May Fair Hotel, and gave him the bad news. He took a philosophical view and, although it was only about eleven o'clock, decided we both needed a drink. All that was available instantly in his room was vodka and ginger ale. Disgusting, but welcome. The difference between Al and Brian was smoothed over, and the production proceeded.

The story of the 'Yellow Submarine' production had a happy ending. The Beatles were persuaded to come to a screening of a rough-cut of the finished film. (They probably by then felt a little guilty, as they had fobbed off the production with three songs, previously discarded, which they considered second-rate, but which in the event worked well enough in the film.) I could see that they enjoyed it and Al, in his element, seized the opportunity to persuade them, success-fully, to make a filmed appearance, as themselves, at the end of the finished feature. This of course enhanced its attraction and it was eventually a great success, winning numerous awards. I took pleasure in telling Al Brodax several years later that I had read that 'Yellow Submarine' was one of Queen Elizabeth's favourite films, which she had had screened several times at Buckingham Palace. Al was highly gratified.

There was a curious postscript, over twenty years later, to my involve-ment with the 'Yellow Submarine' film production. In 1990, I was approached on behalf of the Beatles in connection with the contract which granted to the production company the rights to the music to be used in the film. There were eight parties to this agreement, including the four Beatles, all of whom signed it, and I had signed twice, as a director of both NEMS Enterprises and Subafilms, one of the network of NEMS/Beatles companies which in 1967 had certain rights to performances by them. Litigation was threatened, it appeared, twenty-three years on, over the right of the film distribution company to manufacture and sell video cassettes of 'Yellow Submarine', and my aid was sought to clarify just what rights had, or had not, been granted – video having been barely thought of in 1967. The Beatles' Los Angeles attorneys had not been able, in 1990, to decipher my signature, but it was recognised by a functionary at Apple, by then the centre of the Beatles business. I was duly interviewed in my office in London by one of the attorneys in question, Bert Fields, described in a Vanity Fair magazine article as a 'celebrity lawyer' and the most feared lawyer in Hollywood, whose clients included many of entertainment's top stars. Nothing but the best, and the most expensive, for the Beatles. Mr Fields was agreeable to me, I gave him what information I could, and he told me that I would probably be called as a witness in the case, in Los Angeles.

He also told me that both sides wanted the case decided quickly. Since the civil courts in California were jammed with cases for the foreseeable future it had been agreed that a retired judge would be, in effect, hired for a fee to be split between the parties. His judgment would, I was assured, be binding (and could even be the subject of a bona fide appeal in the courts, if it came to that). I was fascinated by the idea of a 'rent-a-judge'. The case was however settled before such proceedings and I was, on this occasion, spared the ordeal of giving evidence.

The person at Apple who had contacted me was Neil Aspinall, one of the two original Beatles' road managers. I knew him of course from my old NEMS days. He had always been fiercely loyal to the boys from the earliest times, even before Brian Epstein had discovered them. He had stuck to them through thick and thin and they in turn knew they could always rely on him. A somewhat taciturn Liverpudlian he had some accountancy training, which stood him in good stead in their early days. He was by now Apple's managing director in London, still guarding the Beatles' interests.

9
Baby You're A Rich Man

Brian Epstein was determined to spread his wings. Although it was clear that he would always be known as the Beatles' manager he wanted to achieve some form of artistic success in his own right. An opportunity arose for him to acquire a controlling interest in the company which owned and operated the Saville Theatre in Shaftesbury Avenue. Now a cinema, it was slightly out of the West End theatre district, and had never achieved the status of a desirable venue either by performers or by the public. The company was owned by two famous theatre impresarios, Tom Arnold and Bernard (later Lord) Delfont. Arnold and Delfont invited Brian to a meeting at the offices of one of them – I forget which – and I went along too.

The two of them were very flattering to Brian, saying that they were sure his 'magic touch' would ensure the success of any theatrical venture. The proposal, which was accepted after some discussion, was that Brian would acquire from them, through one of our companies, sixty per cent of the controlling company, with Arnold and Delfont each retaining twenty per cent. The theatre had been doing badly so the price we paid was not large but Arnold and Delfont thought they could now sit back and enjoy their shares of the profits which they believed would now come rolling in. Brian Epstein was to have full control of running the theatre, with no interference from the minority shareholders.

Brian set about running the theatre in an unusual manner. During the week it was to function normally, with the usual mix of straight plays, musicals, perhaps a visiting ballet company. But on Sundays Brian decided to mount a series of one-off pop concerts. He himself found the acts, the first of which was one of his favorites, The Four Tops. He had one of the boxes known, as in many theatres, the Royal Box, decorated quite lavishly, with a private sort of drawing room behind it and a private entrance direct from the street. He rejoiced in entertaining selected guests there and sometimes one or more of the Beatles attended. The private entrance was a convenience for them as they were able to avoid the inevitable crowds of fans who would have made their arrivals and departures an ordeal if they had come through the public entrance. I myself attended only a very few of these Sunday shows. I remember in particular the performance of The Cream who were then at the height of their popularity. They created what seemed to be a wall of sound. The kids loved it.

However, for the Saville to be viable as a commercial entity it had to be filled during the week. Initially Brian had plans for this too. He presented 'The Amen Corner', by the American author and playwright James Baldwin. The leading actress was an American, Claudia McNeil, an imposing and friendly lady. We had made a booking for her at a leading West End hotel. This was in 1965. When Miss McNeil arrived in London the hotel suddenly realized that it had overbooked and her room was not available. Nor did accommodation seem to be possible at other similar hotels and so this leading black actress, well known on the American stage, had to make do with a less luxurious hotel in Bloomsbury. She was irritated, but philosophical. The play, which had had a fairly successful Broadway run, was a critical success in London but did not fill the Saville for its six-week season.

I flew to Paris for a couple of nights to see a troupe of dancers from Tahiti who were having success there and wanted to come to London. Their show, at the Theatre des Champs Elysees, was spectacular and

I negotiated for them to come into the Saville for a two-week season. The Saville stage was smaller than that of the Theatre des Champs Elysees, so the spectacle had to be reduced. The presentation involved some waving around of fiery torches, and the London fire authorities stepped in and that too was more carefully controlled. The adapted show was a fair success, but the box office takings did not warrant any extension of the short season. A large part of the problem of keeping the theatre open was that most of the likely successful productions were destined for those theatres controlled by a cartel of theatre owners who had longstanding connections with successful producers. It was impossible, for instance, to secure productions by H.M. Tennant Ltd, controlled by the formidable Binkie Beaumont, as he had deals tied up with his favorite theatres. Bernard Delfont and Tom Arnold were no help, either. Indeed, Brian and I came to realize that they had faced the same problems as we had with the Saville, and that bringing in Brian Epstein was their last hope of bringing the Saville into profit. When they realized that the scheme was not going to work they agreed that NEMS should buy out their remaining forty per cent, leaving us with full ownership. This was not a deal that I rejoiced in, although it was a relief not to have the two of them looking over our shoulders.

We did have a few successes: an Edinburgh Festival production of Shakespeare's 'A Midsummer Night's Dream' was both a critical and a financial success, and a six-week season of the D'Oyly Carte Opera's Gilbert and Sullivan operas resulted in House Full notices. However, a new British musical, 'On The Level', co-presented by Brian Epstein, was not a success with audiences and came off after a few weeks. This was a particular disappointment as it had seemed to have the necessary ingredients for success: the writer Ronald Millar, the composer Ron Grainer, a cast including Barrie Ingham, Gary Bond, Sheila White and Phyllida Law, and the experienced and gifted producer and choreographer Wendy Toye. But as many others have discovered there is no way to guarantee success in a musical.

Having gone to the theatre often in New York, I was accustomed to the practice there of the audience receiving for free the programme to all Broadway shows. This was (and still is) presented in a uniform format, and called the Playbill. At the time we were running the Saville a few, a very few, West End theatres had agreed with the American publishers of Playbill to introduce the same format in their theatres; the programmes were financed by the advertisements in them. When approached, I agreed that the Saville should introduce free Playbills instead of the traditional individual-style programmes. We would be saved the trouble and cost of printing our own programmes, and I believed audiences would like the free Playbills. But the experiment was not a success, the entrenched printers and suppliers of programmes fighting back hard, and the Playbill publishers withdrew from the London scene after a few months' trial.

I had to deal with a particular problem brought to my attention by the Saville's manager, Malcolm Bullock, The Sunday evening performers, nearly all rock 'n' rollers, had to use the same dressing-rooms backstage which were occupied during the week by the performers in the straight productions that were so important for the theatre's survival. Too often the Sunday performers messed up the dressing-rooms, leaving them dirty, strewn with empty bottles and Coca-Cola cans, smelling of pot smoke and sometimes with the actors' possessions damaged. Once an expensive book belonging to an actor, which he had carelessly left in his dressing-room over the weekend, was produced to me with many pages torn out and the cover stained with alcohol. It was an irritating chore to add to the complexities of keeping the theatre going to have to placate the actors and indeed compensate them, while at the same time trying to persuade the rock 'n' rollers to behave decently.

Even Brian could not find enough acts to fill the Saville every Sunday. One day, an American made an appointment to see me in my office to arrange for a Sunday performance. His name was Tony Cox and the performer – who was what would nowadays be called a 'performance artist' – was his Japanese wife, Yoko Ono. We struck the usual deal for a one-night show. It did not prove profitable in view of the slender audience she attracted. I did not attend the show myself – I almost wish I had – but descriptions of it ranged from the surreal to the ludicrous. One 'act', I was told, involved Yoko's inviting members of the audience on stage where they were given fishing rods to try to catch belongings of the remaining audience in the stalls. Possibly, if Mr Cox and his wife had not had the inducement to remain in London for this appearance she might not have met John Lennon. Neither Brian Epstein, John Lennon nor any other Beatle attended her Saville show.

The Saville was in fact a constant drain on the organization's resources but one which could be sustained by the income continuing to be received as management commission from the Beatles' activities, as well those of Cilla Black and some of the other artists in the NEMS stable.

Brian Epstein's visits to America became quite frequent. Much of the business of the Beatles and the majority of the income from record sales and music publishing, as well as their nation-wide tours, came from there, and he found it necessary to have frequent meetings with Walter Hofer, the New York attorney whose office continued to handle many aspects of NEMS's and the Beatles' affairs in the USA. He also met periodically with representatives of Capitol Records urging them to ever more active promotion of the Beatles' recordings. Brian also enjoyed the American way of life, both in New York and in California. Once, when driving with me in the English countryside on a sunny but chilly day in his Bentley convertible, he insisted in opening the top and turning the heater on full blast, saying, "This is very California style!"

Sometimes I went with him to New York and once was able to delight three old friends of mine there by taking them to a Beatles' concert at Shea Stadium, the vast baseball stadium in the borough of Queens. The concert was the usual terrific success, with screaming, happy hordes being kept under some sort of control by large numbers of 'New York's Finest', the city's police force.

My guests at the concert could not know of the tortuous negotiation Brian, myself, our American agents GAC, through their senior vice-president Norman Weiss, and lawyers on both sides of the Atlantic had been involved in concerning, first, the filming of the Shea Stadium concert and, later, its subsequent showing on American television. There was much interest in 'The Beatles at Shea Stadium', which any one of the three US networks, CBS, NBC and ABC would have been willing to secure. The problem was the price we were asking: Brian wanted one million dollars, then an unheard of sum for even an hour-long Special. The more difficult it was to secure such a figure the more adamant he became.

NEMS owned the rights to the film and back in London I took almost daily calls from Norman Weiss, with the amounts being offered always falling short of the magic million, and his protestations that a record-breaking $750,000 was the most that could be secured. Norman was a fine agent and totally honest, so I would relay his calls to Brian with complete confidence in what he was telling us. But Brian, as he told me, was envisaging press headlines such as "Epstein secures record million dollar deal for Beatles' concert on TV". He was insistent that we should hold out. Norman was reaching the end of his tether and finally told me that he had an offer of $800,000 which he was absolutely certain could not be bettered. If we refused it he was certain that we would lose the deal altogether and the show, already in danger of going stale, would remain unseen. I called Brian who was at home in bed and suffering, as I had come to realize, from too many drinks and drugs the night before. He could not take the call, or any other call. I therefore called Norman back at his New York office and accepted the $800,000 on behalf of NEMS, and the deal went through. When I told Brian, he was irritated at first, but did not pursue the matter: his pride would not have allowed him to back down himself from the million dollars, but he was clearly relieved that the much-hyped 'The Beatles at Shea Stadium' would be seen on American network TV, and of course that a huge sum was being paid for it.

My work for the Beatles took me to other parts of the world from time to time. I went to the Bahamas to visit Dr Walter Strach at his house in Nassau. He had been a partner in Bryce Hanmer Isherwood before setting up in the Bahamas, where he was able to assist in handling offshore affairs for some of the firm's clients, including the Beatles. Their second film, 'Help!' was partly filmed there. Walter Strach and his wife were most hospitable and insisted that I stay with them. The temperature was hot and their house was air-conditioned, so I accepted with pleasure. Walter and I worked indoors for some hours and then broke for lunch outside by the pool. There it was baking hot and Walter was forever jumping up and arranging the umbrellas over us to protect us from the sun. To add to the heat Mrs Strach had cooked roast beef and Yorkshire pudding in my honor. I was relieved to get back indoors to work again in the afternoon.

There was no doubt that Brian Epstein was suffering from stress, not helped by his intake of drink and drugs, and his condition was exacerbated by the knowledge that the management contract with the Beatles was due to expire in the autumn of 1967. It seemed likely that it would be renewed, although probably on reduced commission terms: the boys had given up touring, having tired of the strain of traveling – as described earlier by Wendy Hanson – and wanted simply to make their music in the privacy of a recording studio; also, they were showing signs of wanting to handle more of their affairs themselves.

So Brian took two steps to enable him to relax more. The first was the purchase of the house at Kingsley Hill in Sussex. When there he was at his best, relaxed, thoughtful, charming and an excellent host. Soon after my own first visit there he planned a big party as a house-warming and a celebration of the release of what is still considered the Beatles' finest album, 'Sergeant Pepper's Lonely Hearts Club Band'. I was invited of course, and was relieved to be asked to spend the night in the house. I would not have relished driving back to London late at night, and the prospect would have been distinctly inhibiting. The Beatles were invited but only three of them came; Paul, disappointingly, didn't make it. There were many other guests from the world of music and entertainment, including Lionel Bart, Sir John Pritchard, the eminent conductor, and Mick Jagger. Nat Weiss, Brian's lawyer friend, came from New York, and others from Los Angeles. Nat Weiss was not pleased when, quite late on, Brian's devoted secretary Joanne Newfield delicately vomited into a pair of his shoes.

I don't remember much about the party myself. I do recall early in the evening looking out from the house, which was on a small hill, and seeing John Lennon's Rolls Royce winding its way through the country lanes towards the house. It was probably the most distinguishable car in Britain as John had had it painted in gypsy caravan colors – predominantly yellow – and design. I went to bed and to sleep quite early, after having eaten and drunk very well. There were twin beds in the bedroom, and I woke up the next morning to find the late comedian, Kenny Everett, in the other bed. We had no conversation together, as by the time I left the house, in mid-morning, he had not yet surfaced.

**JOHN LENNON'S ROLLS-ROYCE, DECORATED IN GYPSY CARAVAN STYLE,
PHOTOGRAPHED BY GEOFFREY ELLIS AT BRIAN EPSTEIN'S COUNTRY HOUSE,
KINGSLEY HILL**

Brian spent a good part of the next few weeks at Kingsley Hill,
seeming happier, more relaxed and not dependent on his pills. He
learned that I was going to the Glyndebourne Opera one day, not
far from his house, and insisted that I and the friend who had accompanied me, should spend the night at his house. His thoughtfulness
went even further: he found out the timing of the long interval in

the performance and drove over to Glyndebourne to meet us with a picnic in the boot of the Bentley. Later, when we arrived at Kingsley Hill, there was a late-night supper waiting for us. It was just the sort of thing Brian loved arranging, and he enjoyed it as much as we did.

Another instance of his kindness took place when my car broke down in the middle of the Oxfordshire countryside one weekend afternoon. The garage which took it in had no taxis or cars for hire and there were no others locally. The nearest station was ten miles away and all the garage owner could suggest was that I walk three miles to a bus stop, where a bus might eventually appear to take me to a station. I telephoned Brian and an hour or two later a deus ex machina appeared in the shape of his chauffeur in the black-windowed Rolls Royce which he then had. The garage owner was suitably astonished and I arrived home in more comfort than I could reasonably have hoped for.

The other step which Brian took to reduce the strain he was under was at first taken in secrecy. An Australian manager, Robert Stigwood, had been seeing something of him, at first socially: they shared the same tastes for night-life and gambling, and Stigwood, older than Brian, had flattered him by his attentions and his admiration for the younger man's achievements and social position. He had had a somewhat chequered past: it was true that he now had under contract some successful pop acts, the most prominent of whom were the English group Cream (which included Eric Clapton) and the teen idols The Bee Gees. (Originally from the North of England, they had emigrated to Australia, where they had made their name, and had then returned to Britain under Stigwood'd aegis.) During his career, however, Stigwood had his downs as well as his ups and following a bankruptcy his reputation was somewhat tarnished. He had as his financial partner David Shaw, whom I had met while staying with Brian at the Cap-Estel on the French Riviera. Shaw too had been having his problems in the City, with a company called Constellation Investments which provided a tax-saving scheme for high-earners, including pop stars, taking legitimate advantage of a loophole in the tax laws which was later closed by Parliament.

This was the team, Stigwood and Shaw, to whom Brian Epstein agreed effectively to hand over NEMS. He told no one, not the Beatles, not me, not even initially his brother Clive. His plan was to sell fifty-one per cent of the company to Stigwood's company, retaining with the minority interest the personal management of the Beatles and Cilla Black. He would thus be free of administration and most of the existing pressures on him, and able to pursue other interests – a career in television, a film about bullfighting, etc. etc.

The problem was that Stigwood and Shaw did not have the agreed price, half-a-million pounds (a paltry sum compared to offers previously made by more established businesses such as the Grade Organization), and apparently it was not easy to raise. So a further plan was hatched: the Stigwood Organization merged with NEMS and they were given until a date in summer 1967 to come up with the money. The timing was extended by verbal agreement between Brian and Stigwood until a time when the agreement, in the event, became academic.

When the arrangement became known I, like everyone else at NEMS without exception, was surprised and distressed. The same was true of all our close business contacts, such as George Martin and Sir Joseph Lockwood; the latter was particularly appalled as Stigwood had let EMI Records down over a loan made to him shortly before his bankruptcy, a circumstance which had led Sir Joe to declare that he would never again have anything to do with him.

Despite my own shock and disappointment I had some sympathy with Brian, who was clearly desperate to reduce his responsibili-ties. He told me of the deal with Stigwood a few days before it was announced publicly. This was just before Christmas 1966. He and I had kept up our practice of exchanging birthday and Christmas presents but these were always quite modest: I can remember receiving such gifts as a desk blotter, a novelty corkscrew and some LP records. (They were always chosen with care, as he loved giving presents.) When he told me about the Stigwood deal he handed me my Christmas present, which turned out to be a white gold dress watch, way out of our usual expenditure bracket for presents. When I expressed astonishment as well as gratitude, he said, "You mustn't think this is about the Stigwood deal". It was, of course. I always hated the watch and sometime later gave it away myself.

A few days later Brian brought Stigwood and Shaw to the main NEMS office to introduce them to us. Stigwood, whom I found unprepossessing, was wearing a suit of a rather curious material, grey with a windowpane check design. I muttered something about this to Brian, himself immaculate as always, and he said to me "Well, he's nervous too and he bought that suit specially". The day after, Stigwood and his staff moved into the Argyll Street offices; always cramped, they were now full to bursting. Stigwood himself took over my office, with the barest apology, and I was content to occupy a perfectly adequate one at the far end of the NEMS floor. David Shaw had a very small one, previously my secretary's, and their remaining staff settled in wherever they could.

The NEMS people, many of whom comprised those who had come from Liverpool with Brian and the Beatles, were bitterly unhappy but their constant loyalty helped them to make the best of the situation. Vic Lewis was particularly vituperative about Stigwood and Shaw. When the deal was first revealed he urged senior colleagues to resist it. He was unclear how this could be done and I pointed out to him that Brian, as the majority shareholder (none of us, including Vic and myself, had any shares at all), could do what he liked with NEMS Enterprises.

We therefore settled down to try to make the best of what continued to appear a bad job. The whole ethos of the Stigwood people was different from that of NEMS. I once queried David Shaw on how he managed to park his car in the busy street outside for the whole day, and he said that he simply accepted the many parking tickets that accrued and only paid each one when court proceedings were threatened. Not very public spirited, I thought. Fortunately for him this was before the days of wheel clamping. He had an unattractive nervous habit of sucking the end of his tie and altogether failed to inspire confidence, clearly part of the reason for his and Stigwood's failure to raise the purchase price for the majority share of NEMS.

Stigwood himself was not seen much in the office, although it was easy to know when he was there as he too parked his ageing but ostentatious car, a white Rolls-Royce convertible, right outside the building. One day the roof was slashed which made him a little more careful. At a budgeting meeting which I held and which he consented to attend, he was asked for an estimate of the forthcoming year's income from sales of records by The Bee Gees. He responded, simply, "The Bee Gees will sell more records than the Beatles", a non-specific answer which further infuriated the NEMS people.

(One of the artists then under Stigwood's management and who occasionally appeared in the office, was an aspiring young pop singer who called himself Oscar. His father was a well known and exuberant show business lawyer called Oscar Beuselinck, so perhaps his son adopted his name out of filial piety. He achieved little success then but later became famous as Paul Nicholas, much seen in TV situation comedies and on the stage in West End musicals. His father once told me proudly that Paul was to play the title role in the Lloyd Webber and Rice show 'Jesus Christ Superstar'. "Since Paul's going to play the Son of God", said Mr Beuselinck, "just think what that makes me!")

It did not take long for Brian Epstein himself to realize that the merger of the Stigwood organization with NEMS Enterprises was not working. He too became unhappy over trivialities, including the usurping by Stigwood's Rolls Royce of what he deemed to be the parking-space for his own new model Rolls outside the office. More seriously, he was enraged by Stigwood's attempt to hire a yacht for a trip around Manhattan to promote the Bee Gees, then virtually unknown in America, the cost to be borne by NEMS. Brian could himself make ostentatious gestures to promote the Beatles but they were the world's most famous entertainers. He confided in me that he regretted having done the deal with Stigwood, which was having the opposite effect to what he had intended. It was causing more problems than it was resolving. For the time being, however, there seemed to be no way of resolving he situation, although Brian made his displeasure clear to Stigwood, for example over the latter's criticisms of loyal NEMS staff, who as he pointed out had helped to nurture the immense success of the Beatles and other contract artists, including Cilla Black, Gerry and the Pacemakers and Billy J. Kramer and the Dakotas.

In the spring and summer of 1967 no one was happy. Brian Epstein found himself enmeshed in a situation which was not helping him to relieve his complex life. He could not resolve it and sank into further dependence on drugs. Stigwood and Shaw could not raise the money to buy control of NEMS. The staff were bitterly unhappy and frustrated. And the Beatles were flexing their artistic muscles, asserting their individuality and aware that their management contract was about to expire.

I simply did not know what was to happen, which was just as well for my peace of mind.

10
A Day In The Life

It was at the end of August 1967 I went down with fellow guest Peter Brown to spend the Bank Holiday weekend at Kingsley Hill, the weekend that ended so abruptly with Brian Epstein's death at his Belgravia house.

As soon as we heard the news we set off for London. My own car was being repaired and I had hired an unsatisfactory replacement which did not go nearly fast enough for us, but we eventually arrived at Chapel Street. By then, the doctor, John Gallwey – who happened to be my own doctor, summoned as Brian's could not be reached – had been and pronounced Brian dead. No one seemed to know quite what to do, and I made two phone calls. One was to the lawyer, David Jacobs, at his weekend home in Hove, who immediately left and came to the house to assist with the formalities. The other was extremely distressing, to Clive, Brian's brother, in Liverpool. When I told him what had happened and that Brian was dead he screamed down the phone "No, no, it's not true, you're lying". I did what I could to calm him down, myself in a fairly emotional state and he himself had the equally, if not more distressing task of informing his mother.

(The recipients of both these calls subsequently died tragically themselves: David Jacobs an apparent suicide by hanging in the garage of his Hove house; and Clive some years later of a massive heart attack while on a skiing holiday at the early age of fifty-two.)

Those of us assembled at Chapel Street, who included Joanne Newfield, Brian's secretary, and his long-time friend and employee Alistair Taylor, busied ourselves as best we could in discussing arrangements to be made and by telephoning friends and contacts on both sides of the Atlantic. David Jacobs, when he arrived, was a tower of strength dealing with the coroner's office and helping with funeral arrangements. The Epsteins had close relatives in London who of course were informed and who made contact immediately with Queenie Epstein in Liverpool.

Orthodox Jews are on their death, by custom and religion, buried within twenty-four hours. Brian's death was unnatural and there would have to be an inquest. But this was the Sunday of the long Bank Holiday weekend and Monday would be a public holiday, when the Coroner's Court would not be sitting. The inevitable delay was a further cause of anguish to the Epsteins and their relatives. David Jacobs did what he could to minimize the delay and was able to arrange for the coroner's inquest to take place at the earliest possible moment on Tuesday morning.

Back on the Sunday evening, those of us still at Chapel Street had the eerie experience of seeing the news of Bran's death being broadcast on the evening TV news, with a reporter giving the story outside, from the porch of the house. There was much speculation, publicly and privately, about the effect of the news on the Beatles. They were at the time on a highly publicized visit to the Maharishi Mahesh Yogi in North Wales. He was their current guru and Brian had been due to join them there within the next day or two. Peter Brown had telephoned them with the news and spoken to Paul McCartney. The Maharishi soothed them in whatever grief they felt.

At the inquest I was spared from giving evidence since it was Peter Brown who had taken the call from London and had told Antonio, the butler, to break down the door to Brian's bedroom. He therefore gave his evidence, along with Antonio, Dr Gallwey and others, including Brian's regular doctor, Norman Cowan, and the psychiatrist who had treated him for drug dependency. Evidence was also given as to the results of the post mortem examination of the body. The unequivocal verdict was Accidental Death due, said the Westminster Coroner, to an incautious self-overdose. This verdict came as no surprise to those who knew him well. If he had intended to kill himself there would have been no 'incautious self-overdose' just putting him over the edge from life into death, but a massive intake of all the drugs available. Also, despite his problems with the Beatles and his other business worries, he could not have wished to harm his adored mother, Queenie, who had only recently suffered the death of her husband. In addition, he had plans, which were well advanced, to make a series on television in Canada, hosting pop music shows. These he hoped would lead to more recognition of himself as a personality in his own right, no longer in the shadow of the Beatles. Despite these factors and the unequivocal verdict of the Coroner's Court many people, perhaps the majority of those who were interested, persisted in believing that he had killed himself. Many believe it to this day and I was queried about it by the next generation of Beatles fans in America twenty-eight years after the event.

As soon as the verdict was announced and the coroner formally released the body for burial, I made a prearranged telephone call from a public coin-box outside the court to one of Brian's uncles in London, who was able to inform the family in Liverpool that the funeral could go ahead. Brian's body was taken by the undertakers by road from London, and a number of us, including the ubiquitous Nat Weiss who had flown from New York, ourselves made the same journey by train. We went first to the Epstein home, where Queenie Epstein was holding up remarkably well, despite the unmistakable signs of suffering on her face. Words were inadequate, but I joined with the others in expressing our genuine sorrow and sympathy. Among those crowded into the house, along with family, local friends and our party from London, were some of the artists on the NEMS roster: among them was an unnaturally subdued Gerry Marsden and also Cilla Black, who had clearly been weeping. She was dressed in a black outfit with a jacket and rather short skirt over her long, black-stockinged legs. This unfortunately gave her somewhat the appearance of a depressed Principal Boy in pantomime. There was however no doubt of her genuine grief.

The hearse carrying Brian's body was delayed for some time on the road, causing several present to mutter, in an attempt to lighten the atmosphere, "Of course, Brian's late for his own funeral". When it did arrive, we all piled into the waiting limousines and followed the hearse to the family's local synagogue where the rabbi, who knew the Epsteins well, pronounced a blessing. We did not alight from the cars and all the women returned to the house in Queens Drive. According to Jewish custom only men attended the actual inter-ment. The route to the Jewish cemetery took us through some of the most depressing parts of Liverpool. It happened that I and one or two others were in the black-windowed limousine owned by NEMS which was frequently used by the Beatles. There was a factory opposite the gates. The cortege paused at the gates when we arrived in the late afternoon and many of the factory workers, guessing whose funeral it was and believing our car to be carrying the Beatles, swarmed out of the building and started to surround the car excit-edly. We therefore had to get out to show them that we were not the Beatles and to prevent an unseemly riot, and walked the few hundred yards to the grave. After the actual burial we went to a small building where we stood while the rabbi in attendance spoke the appropriate prayers. His following remarks were not appropriate at all. He categorized Brian's death as being symptomatic of the current wave of drug taking and self-indulgence. This caused consid-erable offence to the mourners, who of course included Clive Epstein and a number of his male relatives. We too, friends and colleagues of Brian's, were upset by this less than tactful religious farewell.

The obsequies over, we were about to leave the cemetery when Nat Weiss grabbed my arm. He had with him a small package wrapped in newspaper and explained that it had been given to him the day before by George Harrison on behalf of all the Beatles. It contained a single flower, a chrysanthemum I think, which they wanted placing on Brian's coffin as their own farewell. The difficulty was that flowers are not permitted at Jewish funerals, as I had found myself when enquiring about sending a wreath. Nat was worried about what to do. In the event, we went back to the grave together, where two men were already starting to shovel earth onto the coffin. Fearful that, in deference to Jewish custom, they might prevent the flower being put into the grave Nat, who was himself Jewish, cast the newspaper package unopened onto Brian's coffin, where it was swiftly covered by earth.

There was some comment in the press about the Beatles' absence from the funeral, with insinuations that they were deliberately distancing themselves, or even that they did not care. The truth was that they had wanted to come, but the Epstein family had asked them to stay away, for fear of just the kind of riot that we had narrowly averted outside the cemetery. There was a particularly disobliging reference to their absence in Time magazine and Tony Barrow, the NEMS press officer, with the approval of all of us, including the Beatles themselves, wrote to Time explaining the facts. They had the grace to publish the letter.

I have read that Allen Klein, the New York accountant who had a management arrangement with the Rolling Stones and some other, American, pop acts, heard of Brian Epstein's death on his car radio and that his immediate reaction was "The Beatles are mine". Certainly, he appeared in London shortly afterwards and sought a meeting with Clive Epstein, who by then controlled NEMS Enterprises, and who Klein, without at the time detailed knowledge of the Beatles' contractual situation, presumed had influence over them. Clive was very much a realist and was aware that the Beatles were likely to do exactly what they wished for the future. At the same time, he did not want NEMS to lose whatever interests, managerially and financially, it still had in the boys. Klein had said, in requesting the meeting, that he wanted to discuss a possible joint venture between the Beatles and the Rolling Stones involving a new recording studio. Clive asked me to be present at the meeting. Klein was unaccompanied. The discussion was brief, as he made it clear that his interest in fact was in acquiring the Beatles' management himself and that he would outlay the minimum financial consideration to get it. I was glad when we parted from him as I felt the same sort of antipathy towards him as some people feel in the presence of cats.

Later Klein managed to gain the confidence of, first, John Lennon and his wife, and through them of George Harrison and Ringo Starr. He did a deal with them, although Paul McCartney preferred to put his affairs in the hands of his brother-in-law to be, Linda's brother John Eastman, like his father an attorney in New York. The association with Klein ended in the courts, which did not surprise me.

Allen Klein was not the only person who fancied himself as the new Beatles' manager: Robert Stigwood sought a meeting with them. Whether or not he had by then secured the funds necessary to acquire the controlling interest in NEMS Enterprises, the necessary financing would clearly not be difficult if he could show that he was to be, through NEMS, the Beatles' personal manager, as Brian Epstein had been. The boys consented to attend a meeting, not least I supposed as they were concerned as to their future legal status vis-à-vis the company during the remaining period, albeit short, of their management contract with NEMS. Also, it was clear that they retained some respect for Clive and the Epstein family.

The meeting convened in Brian's old private office at Hille House, Stafford Street. As well as the Beatles, there were present Robert

Stigwood, his partner David Shaw, Clive Epstein and myself. Stigwood did most of the talking, laying out the advantages his management would bring and dwelling at some length on his current success with the Bee Gees, Cream and other acts. He also emphasized his respect for the Beatles' work and their worldwide success, and undertook to carry on Brian's work to the best of his ability.

The reaction was short and not sweet. The Beatles made it clear, reasonably politely, that they wanted no part of him. The principal spokesman was Paul McCartney. He said that no one could replace Brian and that in any event they intended at that time to manage themselves. Stigwood responded that in that case he would not seek to exercise his option to purchase the fifty-one percent of NEMS and that he and the other members of his organization would leave forthwith. The meeting had been brief and I don't recall Clive, David Shaw, myself or the other three Beatles saying anything at all. There was no hanging about for cups of coffee and chat afterwards, but as the Beatles were leaving John Lennon said to me "That'll please Geoffrey, won't it!" I suppose my distaste for the whole Stigwood episode had become well known. While I was glad of John's goodwill I felt at the same time that there were likely to be increasing difficulties with the Beatles in the months to come. In this I was not mistaken.

Clive Epstein felt the same but he was intent for the time being on consolidating what remained of the NEMS Enterprises organization. Although a minority shareholder himself when Brian was alive and a director of the company whom Brian often consulted, principally on financial matters, he had taken no part in the day-to-day running of the company, and rarely came to London from his home and the family business in Liverpool. For this reason, after Brian's death and before his meeting with the Beatles, Robert Stigwood had claimed that he himself should be named Chairman. At the same time, Vic Lewis made it known that he should be made Managing

Director. (Brian had held both positions.) I cannot imagine how the two of them would have got on together in these respective roles. But initially Clive, who by then with his mother held all the shares apart from the ten per cent still owned jointly by the four Beatles, announced that he would assume the chairmanship himself, and named Robert Stigwood and myself as joint Managing Directors. This did not please the former, not least since severe restrictions were put on our powers to expend money: all cheques for over a few hundred pounds had to be signed by Clive or by both managing directors, a restriction not to Stigwood's taste. And above a stated mount Clive alone could sign. He told me that, considering unhappily what would be the best course of action he had consulted the lawyer Arnold Goodman, who had acquired some knowledge of NEMS during the dealings surrounding the stock market flotation of Northern Songs. With his instinct for getting to the heart of things the future Lord Goodman had advised Clive to unscramble the arrangement with Robert Stigwood, of whose then reputation he had no great opinion. This problem was of course resolved by the rejection of Stigwood by the Beatles and his resultant departure.

During all these upheavals life and business had to go on. Brian had been approached a few months earlier by a Hollywood production company, which wanted to secure the services of Ringo to act in a forthcoming film, 'Candy'. Richard Burton was also to appear in it and the producers felt that Ringo, with appropriate direction, could hold his own in such company. In this belief they were influenced by his performances in the two Beatles' films, 'A Hard Day's Night' and 'Help!', particularly the first one in which he had acted alone and convincingly in a lengthy sequence. Brian, with Ringo's consent, had agreed the basic deal and I had subsequently been in contact with the production company's legal and business affairs departments, dealing with the detailed contract and the logistics of Ringo's arrangements to act in the film, which was to be shot in Rome. These negotiations continued with the resumption of business following Brian's death. Finally, I secured Ringo's consent to all the details and the contract was executed. He came to a meeting with me at Hille House, where I was by then occupying Brian's old office, so I could go over all the details with him.

The filming was to take place in early December and when I told Ringo that he was expected to fly to Rome a few days in advance for preparatory work – fittings, rehearsals and so on – he said "OK, but who's coming with me?" It was only then that I realized that with no Brian to accompany him he would feel somewhat lost and uncomfortable in what would be for him an entirely new environment. In the making of the Beatles' films he had been one of four and they had had the usual entourage of road managers, assistants and, not least, Brian himself to make sure all their needs were met and to protect them from unwelcome attention by the production staff and any of the public who could get near them. On the spur of the moment I said, "I'll come with you". I did after all know better than anyone did what Ringo would need to do and what was expected of the film company. He agreed and seemed genuinely reassured. I was very pleased, not just at Ringo's confidence, but because I had never before been to Rome.

Accordingly, a few weeks later, a party of four of us set off from Heathrow Airport: Ringo, his agreeable wife Maureen, Mal Evans, the gentle giant who was one of the Beatles' road managers, and myself. All went smoothly at the airport, where the airline staff had been advised of our party, and on our first-class flight to Italy. It was a different story on our arrival at Rome Airport, where we were greeted by representatives of the film company and by reporters and photographers from the Italian press whom they had alerted. The paparazzi gave us – and particularly Ringo of course – a hard time, but with Mal securing our luggage we managed to get to the car which met us. Part of the deal which I had negotiated was to the effect that Ringo was to have a car and chauffeur exclusively available to him during his stay in Italy, and the producers had honored this obligation by hiring for him a white Rolls Royce. To say that this was conspicuous in Rome would be an understatement and of course it helped in generating publicity for the film to have their unusual star seen in such an exotic vehicle.

We reached the Grand Hotel in good order, although whenever the Rolls was held up in the narrow streets the bystanders would peer in and cry out "Eh, Signor Ringo!" Also, the driver, proud to display his knowledge of English, had an odd way of describing the Roman sights. "This is the famous Condotti Street", he announced, instead of the more normal Via Condotti. At the hotel I had the pleasure of seeing Elizabeth Taylor in close-up when I was having a drink in the bar with Mal Evans. Ringo became friendly with her and Richard Burton during the filming.

The next morning we all four paid a visit to the film studios for Ringo to meet the producer, director and the others involved in the production, and to meet and be photographed with the young female star of the film, Ewa Aulin (who so far as I know subsequently sank back into the Scandinavian obscurity whence she came). For his part as the gardener in the film Ringo had to have his already dark hair dyed black. This did not take long and we left for lunch, with the rest of the day free. I suggested some sightseeing, to which Ringo, Maureen and Mal were agreeable. I asked what they would like to see first. "Well, there's this church", said Ringo in his Liverpudlian drawl. "St Peter's Basilica", I said briskly, and summoned the Rolls.

The driver was delighted to have the opportunity of taking Ringo to such a famous tourist spot and drove the car, by heaven knew what assumed authority, into the very center of St Peter's Square. Tourists abounded, and there was in particular a long line of school-girls entering the Basilica and stretching back into the square. Everyone turned to look at the big white car, possibly wondering if it contained the Pope himself. When Ringo alighted the girls all shrieked and rushed to surround us. (If the Pope had been watching from his window high up in the Vatican, I feel he would have been fairly annoyed.) The girls were brought swiftly under control and our small party went up the steps into the Basilica. I quickly found an English-speaking guide, a middle-aged woman who was probably the only person in Rome, or at least in the Vatican City, who had no idea who Ringo was. As we dutifully followed her round the monuments and memorials the crowd surrounding us grew and grew, eyes fixed on Ringo rather than on the saints, angels and altars, and the guide found herself lecturing to probably the largest, if among the least appreciative, audience of her career as a guide.

We had some more spare time again the next day and decided to start our sightseeing with the Coliseum and then the Forum. However, Ringo sensibly rebelled against going in the Rolls again; it would be convenient for him when he had to go to and from the studios when filming, but it created too much attention when we were going sightseeing. It happened that, never having been to Rome before, I had been given the names and numbers of various people there by friends in London, and one of them was the head of the English Ford concessionaires in Rome. I quickly contacted him and explained the problem. He was all too anxious to help and immediately sent round a Ford Zodiac, adequate for our needs and which we happily used all day. It happened to be white, like the Rolls, but this did not console our driver who compared the Ford unhappily with his beloved Roller all day. But we had a very agreeable day, relatively untroubled by fans and celebrity seekers.

After the first day's filming I decided to return to London, as there were pressing matters to attend to and Ringo was by then comfortably settled in and content to have Mal Evans look after his needs. I was confident that the film company was fulfilling its obligations. The film, when completed was not a great success, but for me the Italian excursion had been a pleasant diversion.

RINGO AND GEOFFREY ELLIS CONFERRING WITH THE
PRODUCERS OF THE FILM 'CANDY' AT THE ROME STUDIOS

I was saddened to learn some years later that Mal Evans had been shot dead by police in Los Angeles. They had raided the house where he was, mistakenly believing it to be occupied by drug dealers. Mal ran out to explain and was immediately shot.

The Beatles had stopped touring, and indeed making any live appearances over a year before Ringo's filming in Rome, their last performance having been in San Francisco at the end of August 1966. Offers for them to appear continued to pour in but all of them were declined. Although they continued to be active in their preferred medium of recording, there was some resentment among their fans and indeed in the public at large (which in fact was much the same thing) that their idols were no longer to be seen live. A letter appeared in the Sunday Times in November 1967 from a correspondent who referred to an offer reported in the press to pay them a million dollars for a single appearance. He wrote that if a manufacturer rejected such an offer for his wares this would have been condemned as unpatriotic and expressed surprise that the Beatles, with their MBEs, had not been criticized. This struck me as unfair comment, so I sought and gained their approval to respond. The Sunday Times accordingly printed the following in their next edition:

"THE BEATLES – Million Dollar Show Myth

"Mr Arthur Abeles in his letter last Sunday concerning a reported offer to the Beatles to earn a million dollars for a one-night stand in New York, states that they 'nonchalantly' turned it down. He asserted that no one had criticized them and that this was a bad state of affairs.

"I would like to make the following points:

"First, no such offer was received by the Beatles or by this company, which manages them. Like Mr Abeles, we read the press reports, but that was all.

"Secondly, experience of organizing appearances in even the largest concert venues in the USA leads us to believe that, if the reported offer had been accepted, a charge of over 10 dollars per head would have been necessary for the promoter to pay his costs and the enormous fee. We would have declined it, since such admission prices seem to us exorbitant and would have led to even greater criticism of the Beatles (not the promoter).

"Thirdly, what artists of any type sing in public – or whether they do at all – is an artistic matter for them to decide and there is no analogy, as Mr Abeles suggests, with a pottery manufacturer turning down an order.

"Finally, the benefit to this country of their receiving a million-dollar fee is problematical in view of the reluctance of the US Internal Revenue Department to recognize, in the face of precedent, that performance fees earned by the Beatles and other pop music artists are taxable in the UK and not the USA.

"Geoffrey Ellis, Joint Managing Director, NEMS Enterprises"

The final paragraph refers to a problem that ran and ran. The outcome did not greatly concern the Beatles, as they were going to be taxed anyway, in one country or the other. But the UK Inland Revenue and the US Internal Revenue Service each spent a great deal of their respective taxpayers 'money trying to get their hands on a share of the earnings of the Beatles and other touring pop groups.

During the time we were running the Saville Theatre the censorship of the Lord Chamberlain was still being exercised over all performances in British theatres. This very grand Court functionary appointed a Licensee to be responsible to him for each theatre, and when NEMS acquired control of the Saville Brian Epstein took over this appointment. After his death I was substituted, and in the winter of 1967 I was summoned to St. James's Palace to give an account of activities at the theatre during the preceding year, in contemplation of the renewal of his licence for the next. If the licence were withdrawn the theatre would have to close. I accordingly presented myself at the palace at the appointed mid-morning hour on a cold, damp and misty November day. I was received by a footman and offered in the anteroom to the Lord Chamberlain's office a glass of mulled wine, a huge silver bowl of which was steaming on a table. I gratefully accepted this welcome antidote to the bitter weather. Lord Cobbold, the then Lord Chamberlain, was most courteous and friendly when my turn came to be interviewed. I had thought that the meeting would be purely a formality but he had on his desk full information concerning the shows that had been presented at the Saville during the year, including the Sunday evening pop concerts. He also had press cuttings describing the riotous behavior of some of the audiences for these. He took me gently to task over these scenes of misbehavior and I had to assure him that we would do our best to control the audiences at any future concerts of this type.

The licence was renewed, and it was at about this time that the eminently respectable D'Oyly Carte Opera Company came to the Saville for a second six-week season with their repertoire of Gilbert and Sullivan operas. During their run the Queen, with the Duke of Edinburgh and the Prince of Wales, came to a performance in aid of a theatrical charity of which she was Patron, and I had the pleasurable duty, as Lord Chamberlain's licensee of the theatre, of welcoming her outside the theatre and conducting her inside to meet the chairman of the charity and other functionaries. (Queenie Epstein witnessed this in the foyer and I felt sad for her that it was I and not Brian who was performing this duty.) The men bowed their heads in the customary manner and the women made their bobs. The chairman's wife, however, who was wearing a long and elaborate evening dress, on being presented to Her Majesty sank into a full court curtsey before her, beautifully executed. Everyone looked a little surprised, a little amused, but the Queen accepted this tribute with her customary grace.

Some weeks later I received from a friend who happened to have been in Tokyo at the time a cutting from an English language newspaper published in Japan which had a photograph of the royal party arriving at the Saville; no doubt the Tokyo newspaper was interested as the performance was of 'The Mikado'. The caption to the photograph described the event and Her Majesty's attendance, and added: "The man at the right was not identified". Me.

THE AUTHOR GREETS QUEEN ELIZABETH AND PRINCE CHARLES AT THE
SAVILLE THEATRE, NOVEMBER 1967

Very soon afterwards the Lord Chamberlain's authority over theatre performances was abolished by law. Nudity on stage had always been forbidden by him (except in very circumscribed conditions), and I was in the audience at the opening night of 'Hair', the American musical in which the performers, male and female, stripped naked on stage. There were rumors, no doubt fostered by the producers for their publicity value, that the police might raid the theatre and make arrests on the grounds of indecency but we, and the performers, were spared any such drama.

11
Magical Mystery Tour

During 1967 the Beatles had been planning to make a film, produced by themselves and under their total control, and had discussed this project with Brian Epstein before his death at the end of August. The prime mover was Paul McCartney and it was he who persuaded the others to go ahead in the autumn. This was to be the 'Magical Mystery Tour' film, to be screened initially on television. Needless to say, the filming attracted enormous publicity, not least because much of it took place out of the studio in various parts of Southern England, where sightseers were not lacking.

What the status of NEMS would have been had Brian been still around I do not know. The management contract was ending, but the fact that Brian had been consulted indicated that there would have been some involvement by the company, which one naturally hoped would be profitable. In the event, I was pleased to learn that NEMS was to be the distribution agent, on a normal commission basis. Given the curiosity value of the film, even before it was made, and the universal belief at the time that the Beatles could do no wrong and that anything they produced would be as first-class and commercial as their records it was reasonable to anticipate a substantial income from its distribution. Placing the 'Magical Mystery Tour' in Britain presented no problem: it was eagerly snapped up by the BBC, to be shown on Boxing Day when it would catch the enormous family Christmas audience. Color TV sets were still quite rare, and most of the audience would see it in black and white.

The major income would come, in the normal course of events, from America and quite early during the making of the film in the late autumn – including Ringo, whose filming in Rome of 'Candy' did little to interrupt the schedule – three US bidders emerged. One was a famous manufacturer of household appliances, whose interest was in sponsoring the film on TV and thereby gaining in the public's estimation from the association with the Beatles; another was one of the major American advertising agencies, wishing to secure the rights to the show to sell on to its clients; and the third was one of the three major networks itself, anxious to have the production to boost its ratings. The network, although it had an office in London, deemed the project of sufficient importance to send from New York one of its vice-presidents in charge of programming to gain what knowledge of the production he could and to engage in preliminary negotiations. I was only too happy to meet him and discuss terms, but the Beatles were adamant that neither he nor other bidders could be present at the actual filming. They wanted the film to be finished and as perfect as they could make it before any outsiders saw it. They worked very hard at it, Paul in particular taking endless trouble over the editing.

'Magical Mystery Tour' was duly screened by the BBC to a huge audience on Boxing Day. I had already seen it, more than once, in various forms and finally in the edited version and, despite my mistrust of my own reaction to the Beatles' music and other activities, had serious misgivings as to its quality and acceptability to the mass audience. It seemed to me amateurish and, although much of the Beatles' popularity in the 'sixties was due to their always appearing to take themselves less than seriously, I felt that their first self-made production ought to be totally professional, if only to justify the popular belief that they could take on and beat the real professional film and TV producers at their own game. The acting and direction were often sloppy, and there was the notorious flash of female breasts, then unheard of – and certainly unseen – on TV to be reckoned with.

The BBC was unhappy but bowed to Paul's insistence that they not be edited out.

The critical reaction was poor and in this instance justified my misgivings. In a way it was inevitable that at some stage the critics would turn against the Beatles after so long a period of slavish adulation, but it seemed a pity that this had to happen just when they wanted to prove that their talent was all their own and owed little to management or production by others. On the other hand, some of us felt a measure of satisfaction at this proof that Brian Epstein had been the necessary guiding hand to the boys' activities. He certainly would not have allowed the film to be shown in the state in which it was seen by a disappointed British public.

Clearly, the panning the 'Magical Mystery Tour' received from the British press was not going to help in the matter of an American sale, and I set off for New York in January in none too hopeful a frame of mind. There I was met by Walter Strach, who had come up from the Bahamas to assist and, in particular, to advise on the handling of the hoped-for large dollar sums which would accrue from US television sales. I had appointments to show the film to the three bidders. I don't recall in what order they saw the production but I do remember carrying the can of film (this was before the days of video cassettes) from one office building to another, each organization having its own screening room and of course its own team of executives privileged to attend the showing. I sat in with the people concerned at the first screening, but at the subsequent two – spread over a couple of days – I simply couldn't bear to watch it, or sustain the embarrassment of observing the disappointed reaction of each separate audience. Indeed, after each screening, the senior person present informed me, unnecessarily, that there might be some problems, they would have to discuss the matter among themselves and that they would be in touch in due course. In other words, 'Don't call us, we'll call you'. In each case, too, the question of the breasts was raised, it being indicated quite clearly that it would be impossible to screen the film on American TV unless they were edited out. In each instance, anxious to save a remotely possible sale, I said I would take back their comments to the Beatles, while knowing what their reaction would be. The upshot was of course no deal.

It was snowing in Manhattan in those January days and icy cold. When Walter Strach – who had himself been disappointed by the film – and I emerged from the third and final screening it was the rush hour and people were stumbling along sidewalks packed with snow while fighting the blizzard. I had no limousine at my disposal, not wishing to expend money unnecessarily on what I had suspected in advance would be a futile mission, and it was impossible to find an empty taxi. I vividly recall taking the slow bus ride up Madison Avenue to our hotel, standing in the packed interior clasping the can of film under my arm and wondering what the other passengers would think if they knew what it contained – and how incredulous they would be if they knew it was a new Beatles' film, although one already destined to be a flop.

Eventually, 'Magical Mystery Tour' was shown in America, but some time later on, on a few syndicated TV stations, not on network TV. It subsequently became something of a cult item on the US college circuit and has finally attained something approaching respectability, mainly as a curiosity. There was also considerable consolation in the fact that the record of the new songs composed for the film had performed just like all other Beatles' records and shot to the top of the charts. Their record-buying public, at any rate, remained faithful and the record royalties continued to pour in.

I had some other items of business to attend to during that New York trip and then had to return to London with the disappointing news. As for Walter Strach, he went back to Nassau without the prospect of further heaps of dollars coming in from this particular venture. In addition, it happened that Arnold Goodman strongly advised Clive

Epstein, during their consultation concerning the Stigwood problem, to arrange for NEMS to repatriate to the UK all the funds being held by Walter Strach's operation for the account of the Beatles, and this was done as swiftly as possible.

A constant worry at this time was the Saville Theatre which continued to lose money at an alarming rate. There seemed to be no future for it in NEMS's hands and Clive was anxious to get rid of it. We approached numerous theatre owners and investors but none was prepared to take it on. We had estimates to convert it into a cinema, but these proved too expensive. Finally, we went back to Bernard Delfont, who with Tom Arnold had originally lumbered us – as I by then saw it – with this jinxed theatre, which had never been successful, part of the reason being that it was in the wrong part of Shaftesbury Avenue. Delfont was, predictably, unenthusiastic but he saw the opportunity for a potentially profitable deal. After his accountants had pored over the disastrous figures he agreed to reac-quire the lease from NEMS, but for this he required a substantial payment to cover the losses. He thus got the property back and received a large sum of money for doing so. I felt even more sympathy for the Epsteins in the face of such dealings in the wake of Brian's death, and that of his father, too.

Eventually, some years ago now, the theatre was converted into a cinema, or rather several cinemas, and the Saville is now forgotten and unmourned.

During the next few months, the first half of 1968, I was kept busy, partly assisting Clive Epstein to restructure NEMS Enterprises and partly dealing with problems thrown at us by new advisors taken on directly by the Beatles. While relations remained perfectly amicable on a personal basis, new lawyers, film producers and record producers directly employed by them sought to prove their worth, and their superiority to previous management, by querying many aspects of Brian Epstein's contracts negotiated on the Beatles' behalf.

These ranged from the recording contract and such obvious targets as the merchandising deals to relatively small matters. An instance was the perfectly normal contract entered into with the writer of what was to be an authorized biography of the Beatles: in exchange for their co-operation with him and consenting, each one, to be interviewed in depth, they were to receive a hefty proportion from advances and royalties earned by the book, sure to be a bestseller. The arrangement was, as I say, perfectly normal. However, a lawyer now employed, not retained, by the Beatles sought to renegotiate the contract, insisting that they be entitled to a much larger share of the income. This seemed to me to be hardly fair, since all the work was to be done by the writer, himself well-known, and it became necessary to insist on upholding the original contract. This episode produced a strange sensation in me as I was for the first time acting, as it were, against the Beatles' interests. But I felt sure that this was right and that the contract originally agreed with Brian deserved to be upheld. In due course, the various new advisors were dispensed with, but not before large amounts were spent by the Beatles on offices, salaries and other expenses.

NEMS continued for a time to help out. John Lyndon, the efficient presenter of shows, was seconded to help the famous, or notorious, Apple shop in Baker Street, central London. He despaired of the sloppy administration and one day called to urge me to come over to the shop that afternoon. The Beatles had taken the decision, he told me, to close it down and give away all the stock. The public was to be allowed in the next day to take whatever they liked but that evening staff, friends and business associates were able in advance to help themselves. I could not get there myself but John kindly grabbed a couple of silk scarves for me, one of which I still have.

Although NEMS continued to manage some of the remaining artists, the heart had gone out of the company with Brian's death and the virtual defection of the Beatles. Cilla Black, too, was on the point of departing, to be excellently managed by her long-time boyfriend,

Bobby Willis, who had in any case been acting as her road manager and general factotum during her years with NEMS. That he was more than capable of taking over is evidenced by her immense continuing popularity, matched no doubt by her earnings. As an enduring star of the entertainment business, she has probably proved as much of a tribute to Brian Epstein's flair in discovering and managing her as have the Beatles. On the other hand, neither Brian nor Bobby could make her a star in America. Cilla and Bobby were happily married for many years, until his death a few years ago.

While NEMS continued to have rights to commission on much of the Beatles' income, rights which existed under contracts negotiated and executed before Brian Epstein's death and the expiration of their management contract – and rights which were in major instances contested by their new advisors – there was no-one to discover and bring in new acts. No one at NEMS, myself included, really expected this and so the major part of the business became an agency, booking appearances and tours for the existing contract artists and others. Vic Lewis, with his agency experience, became the managing director of this side of the business, which for a time flourished reasonably well. He removed the large color TV set to his office from Brian's Chapel Street house – then still quite a novelty – which Brian had acquired through the company, and prevailed upon Clive to agree to the purchase of a Rolls Royce for his use.

But all the time Clive had in mind divesting himself of an unwelcome responsibility. This he eventually and not without difficulty achieved. Before that time arrived he and I had agreed that I should leave: I had no interest in the agency and was not the person to build up any new pop music management. By then, too, I had had enough of the sniping from the Beatles' new regime. (In due course I got considerable satisfaction when each of the new advisors fell by the wayside. None could replace Brian and the rest of us.) So, in June 1968, with goodwill on both sides and a reasonable compensatory cheque in my pocket, I resigned my directorships in the various NEMS companies, and left.

The fortune left by Brian Epstein on his death was not as large as might have been expected. He had lived extravagantly, with his town house, his country house, his servants and cars, his traveling, his entertaining and his gift giving. He died intestate, so that all he possessed passed to his mother, Queenie. She, however, with her surviving son Clive behaved with exemplary generosity and thoughtfulness.

Brain had in fact drafted a will sometime earlier, at a time when he had apparently felt somewhat suicidal. But on recovering his spirits he did nothing to formalize or execute it. It was, however, found among his papers and Queenie and Clive proceeded to carry out his wishes. Queenie asked to see me, came to tea in my flat and gave me a generous cheque. "Out of Brian's money", she said. She did the same for one or two others who had been close to him and who were mentioned in the draft will. Clive asked me to choose an object from Brian's possessions, and I took a handsome late eighteenth-century leather-topped desk table, which had been in the elegant drawing room in Chapel Street.

While I was looking round the room for the last time I mentioned how much I admired a painting by L.S. Lowry hanging on one of the walls: it was, ironically, a bleak picture of a graveyard under snow. Clive, thinking that I might be going to ask for it – it was I knew too valuable for this possibility – hastily said that he and his mother, knowing how much Brian too had liked and valued it, were giving it to John Lennon. The other three Beatles received similarly valuable mementoes and a few of Brian's other friends were, like me, invited to choose something to remember him by.

Over the following months and years I was curious, and indeed surprised, at how many people believed that Brian Epstein had committed suicide. This was certainly a common belief among people I met both socially and in business. Apparently, suicide seemed in many people's minds to have been the logical end to his life and it was clear that many preferred not to believe the coroner's verdict of Accidental Death. A number of writers perpetuated in their works the belief in his suicide, but one former friend and colleague wrote of 'the open verdict', which was simply nonsense.

I wrote to a few of the more responsible authors, pointing out the coroner's verdict, and that the suicide myth was hurtful to Brian's family and friends. I also referred to it as an instance of what was written, often erroneously, becoming in due course accepted as historical fact. The well-known author and journalist Christopher Booker wrote back to me apologizing for his mistake and had the reference corrected in a future edition of his work. Lord Goodman who, twenty-six years after Brian's death, wrote in his memoirs published in 1993 how nice he had found Brian Epstein at the time of the Northern Songs stock market flotation, but that on observing John Lennon's and Paul McCartney's behavior he was not surprised that he had committed suicide. He too promised in a letter to me to arrange for a correction in any future edition, but himself died before this could be done. The oddest response came from the writer Brian Masters: while accepting that the verdict had been one of Accidental Death he appeared in his letter to me to be justifying his reference to Brian's 'suicide' in a book of his by saying that what people believed to be true was in fact the real history. I could not follow his reasoning, but he too agreed that his work should be corrected.

In 1983, Peter Brown, who had been Brian Epstein's personal assistant at the time of the death and had stayed on with the Beatles for some time in their Apple organization, co-wrote with an American pop music journalist a book about the Beatles, their lives and loves. They interviewed many of us who had been involved, although implying that the book was to be about the 'Swinging London' of the 'sixties, rather than an intimate look at the Beatles. The book was published first in America and I happened to be in New York when copies appeared in bookstores there. I bought one and checked the index for references to myself. These all appeared to be quite harmless and I was amused to read Peter Brown's assertion that Robert

Stigwood had complained to Brian Epstein about some of the NEMS employees, no doubt including myself, when he was working in our offices. This seemed to me perfectly reasonable, since I on my side had not concealed my disapproval of him.

On later reading the book in detail I was irritated to note numerous errors of fact, some of them quite trivial. Brian Epstein's first London flat was described as being in Williams Mews, while on another page it was called, first, the Wadham House flat, and a few lines later the Whadham Street flat. The actual address was Whaddon House, William Mews. Clive Epstein was called Brian's elder brother, whereas he was two years younger. Hille House, the location of Brian's private office, was spelled phonetically as Hilly House, and the town of Hounslow came out as Houndslow. These inaccuracies – and there were many others – did give rise to doubt as to the veracity of the authors' tales of the Beatles' private lives.

Wendy Hanson was angry at Peter Brown's stating that he had come to London specifically to take up the job of Brian's personal assistant, whereas she had held that position at the time and he had succeeded to it only after she resigned, over a year after he had arrived from Liverpool.

A good many years later I was amused to see Peter Brown on American TV criticizing the biographer Kitty Kelley for numerous factual inaccuracies in her book about the British royal family. His comments were perfectly fair, but the words pot, kettle and black did spring to mind.

I was surprised to find my name in a footnote in Peter Brown's book which was not referred to in the index, presumably as it was an afterthought. I was said to have done something which I ought not to have done – or, to be more precise, not to have done something which I ought to have done. This was not true and I wrote to Peter Brown right away enclosing documentary evidence. Receiving no reply, I instructed my lawyers some weeks later to write to the publishers in New York requesting a correction. After lawyerly correspondence with the publishers' legal department a document was drawn up and signed by all the parties, Peter Brown, his co-author, the publishers and myself, agreeing that the damaging reference should be deleted from further editions of the book, including in paperback and publications abroad. This obligation was honored and the British edition has no footnote. My solicitors had advised that I could sue for damages on the grounds that my business reputation had been damaged, but this was the last thing I, bearing in mind my experience of litigation in New York, wished to do. I just wanted the record of my involvement with the Beatles in the 'sixties to be truthful.

Over thirty years on, the achievements of Brian Epstein and his small band of helpers appear all the more remarkable. With the perspective of these years one can regard with astonishment how the talents of the four Beatles, of Cilla Black and of some of the others were discovered and nurtured by what was little more than a group of young amateurs. Those of the NEMS Enterprises Ltd employees who already did have some experience of the entertainment business – Tony Barrow, the pop record reviewer, Bernie Lee, the concert booker, John Lyndon, the stage presenter and one or two others – had not held the most senior positions in the business before. Others, certainly including myself, had no previous knowledge whatever of the arcane ways of the music business world, its curious contracts and the division of responsibilities between publishers, record companies, producers, managers, promoters and agents, all aiming to profit from the creators and performers. Brian Epstein himself was experienced only in the commercial end of the record business and knew little if anything of what lay behind the finished products he was selling when he first saw and approached the Beatles and offered to manage them.

PAUL McCARTNEY CHATTING WITH GEOFFREY ELLIS AT A LUNCH HELD IN 1989 TO CELEBRATE THE 75th ANNIVERSARY OF THE PERFORMING RIGHT SOCIETY. BEHIND GEOFFREY IS MICHAEL FREEGARD, THEN CHIEF EXECUTIVE OF THE PRS

Despite these tremendous disadvantages and the frankly ramshackle nature of the NEMS organization, and despite unsatisfactory help from some professional advisors, we managed to build and sustain the reputation, and both the artistic and commercial success of the Beatles during the greatest period of their success as a group. During the years 1964 to 1968 they were without a doubt the biggest stars in entertainment throughout the world. In that period they changed the nature of popular music, they influenced the way people looked and thought, and they narrowed the gap between the generations in the Western world.

12
Only A Northern Song

At the time I left NEMS I had no idea what I was going to do next. During the period when Stigwood seemed likely to take the company over I had talked to George Martin about the possibility of my joining his burgeoning and increasingly successful A.I.R. organisation. They had recording studios in central London and were specialising in music used in commercials. However, in the turmoil following Brian Epstein's death I felt that I could not leave NEMS until Clive had had a chance to resolve the many problems that he faced. He needed my help, so I told George that I would have to stay for the time being. Eventually, I was able to leave with a clear conscience.

The first thing I did was to go on holiday to Italy. I went with Wendy Hanson to the Spoleto festival, where I met many of her friends from the classical music world, including the festival's founder, Gian-Carlo Menotti, for whom Wendy had previously worked, and his companion, the American composer, Samuel Barber. Wendy and I went to many concerts, recitals and a performance in the small opera house of Wagner's 'Tristan and Isolde', sung by unknown soloists with the accompaniment of the Zagreb Radio Symphony Orchestra. I thoroughly enjoyed the change from the turmoil I had been experiencing in London.

Back there, Wendy introduced me to a young and energetic photographers' agent named David Puttnam. After some discussion, we agreed that I should join him in a venture he was planning, to produce initially some low budget films. We were financed to start with by James Garrett & Partners, a very successful company producing TV commercials. The eponymous owner was very supportive and David's fertile mind spawned numerous ideas for promotional and other films. We had offices in Farm Street, Mayfair, and all that was missing was any commission actually to make a film.

As it happened, much of my time was taken up with long discussions on the telephone about Northern Songs, the public company that published all Lennon and McCartney's output. I had remained a director of it after leaving NEMS, at the request of Dick James, whose Dick James Music still administered it. Clive Epstein was also a director, along with Dick and his business partner, the accountant, Charles Silver. Dick and Charles, who were full-time directors, while Clive and I were strictly part-time, had become increasingly concerned over the current activities of the Beatles, especially of course John and Paul, under the influence of their new advisors such as the American Allen Klein. John and Paul had a commitment to write a given number of new songs a year, all to be assigned to Northern Songs. (It may seem strange to some that creative talent could be harnessed in this way by legal contract but the practice is common in the music business, though enforcement varies according to circumstances.) The composers continued to receive not only their hefty royalties from the licensing of their works for the purposes of recordings, by the Beatles themselves and by the literally hundreds of other artists who also recorded their songs, and from all performances, live and on radio, film and television, but also the benefit of the ever-increasing value of their shareholdings in Northern Songs and the dividends which they produced.

Despite the apparent stability of Northern Songs and its continuing success on the stock market Dick James was worried, as he told us at our regular board meetings. He felt, not without reason, that the

Beatles' new advisors, anxious to prove themselves on all fronts, were likely to mount some sort of attack on the company. This, he theorized, might be by insisting on a much higher royalty rate to boost John's and Paul's incomes, coupled with the threat that if this was not agreed the two would stop writing songs until the expiration of their contract. The resultant non-fulfillment of their commitment of a minimum of songs annually would be an added complication. Such a threat did not in fact materialize, but Dick had a more specific worry. John Lennon was now married to Yoko Ono, who was a songwriter of sorts herself, and John was claiming that she shared in his own composing, with the copyright in her half share being assigned to her own company. There was the threat also, which later materialized, that Paul McCartney would likewise co-write in the future with his new wife, Linda Eastman, with her half share in their joint compositions likewise not going to Northern Songs. These arrangements, about which it must be said the board was highly skeptical, would have the effect of diluting considerably the income of Northern Songs and hence its profitability. The shareholders, thousands of them, financial institutions as well as individual fans and other investors, would not be happy. And Dick was one of the largest shareholders himself. What was more, his relationship with his star writers had completely broken down. He never saw them, rarely if ever even spoke to them on the telephone and was not welcome at their recording sessions. The only contact with them was the furnishing of the songs themselves, together with an assignment contract for each one which John and Paul assiduously signed, entitling them to their royalties.

Accordingly, Dick James hatched a plot with his accountant partner Charles Silver, who was Chairman of Northern Songs; Dick was Managing Director. They would secretly enter into an agreement to sell their substantial shareholdings to a third party who would thereupon make an offer for all the remaining shares, including of course John's and Paul's. If John and Paul were the only ones not to accept what would be a lucrative offer they would remain as minority shareholders only, with no influence at all over the handling of their immensely valuable copyrights. (As it happens, the same would be true if they did accept, but they would have the consolation of a large, though by now taxable, capital gain.) I regret to relate that neither Dick James nor Charles Silver informed me, or my co-director Clive Epstein, of their plan in advance, although I have no doubt that it should have been discussed by the full board. Nor, equally important, did they tell John Lennon and Paul McCartney, rightly fearing that if they did so John and Paul would do all in their power to scupper the deal.

The chosen purchaser of the shares was ATV, Associated TeleVision, headed by the redoubtable Sir Lew (later Lord) Grade, brother of Bernard (Lord) Delfont. Grade had been Dick James's agent when Dick was a singer, and the two had maintained sporadic contact, with a certain amount of mutual respect for each other's business success over the years. Dick told me that Lew Grade had once or twice made more or less informal offers to him for "the Beatles' publishing", and to Dick he now appeared the obvious purchaser. The deal was that ATV would buy Dick's and Charles's shares, totaling something under forty per cent of the equity, for an agreed price, and would then offer to buy all the remaining shares for the same price. If and when ATV owned Northern Songs, it would continue to be administered by Dick James Music for another year or two, for an administration fee of ten per cent of gross income – in fact continuing the existing arrangement – with Dick remaining as Managing Director.

A minor aspect of the deal agreed with Grade was that the current directors would remain on the board after the take-over by ATV, together with nominees to be appointed by Grade. I still however, have a copy of a letter written by ATV's solicitors, after all the dust had settled, requiring in somewhat formal terms that at the next board meeting of Northern Songs the resignations of Clive Epstein and Geoffrey Ellis would be "dealt with". This had been so poorly prepared that the names of the ATV nominees to be substituted for us had not been inserted before the letter was sent, with a space for a name left blank. He was to be a representative of the Beatles, doubtless hard for ATV to find at that juncture. When Clive and I expostulated at this treatment, in clear breach of the prior undertaking, we each received a coolly polite letter signed by Lew Grade expressing appreciation of our past services and regretting the necessity of our being asked to step down. In truth, I was by then relieved no longer to have this responsibility, as I was moving on. But Clive felt deeply the severing of this link with such a successful company, which his brother Brian had had so great a part in founding.

While I was still a director I was kept fully informed of the developments which followed Dick James's agreement with Lew Grade. Dick managed to have a private meeting with John and Paul to explain the deal with Grade. They were outraged, first because they had not been advised in advance and as a corollary that they had not been given the opportunity to buy the shares themselves. Dick believed, rightly, that they would not have been able at that time to raise the money needed for this purpose, and he wanted a quick deal. In this he was disappointed since the Beatles, guided by Allen Klein, mounted a counter-offer. This was a complicated affair, whereby they would buy only four out of seven shares owned by each holder, or two out of seven if they were able to secure all those already committed to ATV (i.e. Dick's and Charles's); in either case, enough to give them control, but not complete ownership of the company.

My own somewhat invidious position as a director of a company which was being attacked by the Beatles, to whom I still felt the loyalty which came with the link to Brian Epstein, gave me some concern. Any conflict was resolved by my enforced resignation from the board, another reason why I was not too concerned at that juncture.

There was a further complication arising from the emergence of a consortium of City interests to buy all the shares – a complication noted with delight by the press, which monitored the tussle for control of Northern Songs during the many months which it lasted. There was also, we learned, dissension within the ranks of the Beatles and their advisors. Paul was taking advice from his brother-in-law to be, John Eastman, the New York lawyer and son of the formidable Lee Eastman, one of the best-known American music business attorneys. The younger Eastman had an Ivy League appearance and manner which contrasted with the down to earth approach of Allen Klein, who was behind the Beatles counter–offer for the Northern Songs shares.

Eventually, Lew Grade's ATV won the fight, beating off the Beatles' unusual offer with some support from the City consortium. Dick and Charles got their money, although they alone received an amount based on their original deal with Lew Grade. All the other share-holders benefited from the increase in ATV's offer subsequently forced on it in the course of the battle for control.

The conclusion of the takeover and my departure from the board of Northern Songs coincided with the anniversary of my rather loose employment by Corpro, the name we had devised for David Puttnam's film production venture, and he and I agreed that things had not at that juncture turned out as we had hoped. We therefore agreed that we should part, most amicably, and I wished him all the success which he eventually achieved; although even then I could not envisage his prominence as the producer of 'Chariots of Fire' and other wonderful films, as the head for a time of one of the biggest Hollywood studios and as Lord Puttnam, a leading light under the Labour government and an inspiration to many.

Dick James asked me to come and see him and Charles Silver. They told me that although they had considered during the past year, since I had left NEMS, offering me a position at Dick James Music, it had not seemed to them appropriate to do so while I was a director of Northern Songs, a public company prior to the ATV take-over. The situation had now changed and, in addition, Charles, who had been the business brains behind Dick James Music since its inception, had had a leading role in all the affairs of Northern Songs as its chairman and had given up his position as senior partner in the accountancy firm of Silver, Altman & Co to devote himself full-time to these interests, was now feeling the strain of his involvement, particularly over the previous months. He wanted to take life more easily and he and Dick hoped therefore, that I would come and take over much of the administration and contractual work from him. I accepted with little hesitation as I had come to know Dick well and to respect him. I was also by then very interested in the music publishing business. I had considered while at NEMS that the publishing of Lennon and McCartney's music, and that of some others managed by us then, by Dick James was the most professionally handled part of those artists' activities. So I was attracted by the idea of being more directly involved with the publishing world.

Having therefore negotiated a reasonable remuneration package with Dick I agreed to start work almost immediately at the New Oxford Street offices of Dick James Music, or DJM as it was generally known. These offices were not far away from Denmark Street, the traditional 'Tin Pan Alley' of popular music, where Dick had himself started out in business in a two-room office only a few years previously.

Quite soon after I joined DJM Charles Silver retired completely. He had felt deeply the strain of the takeover of Northern Songs and by then was not robust physically. Sadly, he died not long afterwards. I moved into his pleasant office, which had been conveniently located for him next to the company's busy accounts department. From time to time, as I came and went from my office to Dick James's, where we had very frequent discussions and meetings with writers and business associates, I encountered some of the songwriters contacted to DJM who would come in to collect their royalty cheques or to raise queries about amounts, sources of income, and sometimes to request advances or loans. A regular, generally weekly, visitor was a young, up-and-coming composer who wrote under the name Elton John.

13
How Do You Do It?

Elton's real name was Reginald Kenneth Dwight, and his pseudonym – which eventually became his legal name by deed poll – was a tribute to two musicians he admired, Elton Dean and John Baldry ('Long John Baldry'), with whom he had worked. Elton, who wrote only music, not words, was some times accompanied into the DJM office by his lyricist and friend, Bernie Taupin. They would come to collect their weekly advances. I think Elton initially received £10 a week, later increased to £15, to help with living expenses while he and Bernie were living with Elton's mother, Sheila, and his stepfather, Fred Farebrother, in the London suburb of Pinner. The total of these advance payments would be deducted from royalties earned when these eventually came in. Of course, in the case of some hopeful song-writers such advance payments would never be recouped, but Dick James considered them business investments and such losses would be outweighed by successes such as Elton's.

Elton was shy, but friendly and we would always exchange a few words when our paths crossed in the accounts department. Although I had little to do with the artistic side of DJM I naturally became aware of the enthusiasm for Elton and Bernie's songs and the excitement engendered by the increasing sales of Elton's records. Dick James had great confidence in him and had signed him up for his recording, publishing and management. So far as the latter was concerned DJM took the commission normal in the business of 25% on receipts from Elton's live performances, on stage and on radio and television, but none from his recording and publishing, since DJM was itself the publisher and Elton's records were produced by the in-house production company, This Record Co, and released on the DJM record label. 'This' was said to be an anagram of 'Hits', although so far as recordings by some other artists were concerned another anagram of the word was bandied about.

Quite early in Elton John's career with DJM, Dick James took a considerable risk and financed a trip to America, first to Los Angeles where he took the Troubadour Club on Santa Monica Boulevard by storm. When his success there was repeated in New York Dick himself, unaccustomed for all his experience in the music business, first as singer himself then as publisher, to the role of manager to a star, flew to the city to surprise Elton by congratulating him in person. Elton was in fact a big star in the States before he really hit the big time at home in Britain.

His progress was followed with great excitement by all the staff at the DJM offices in New Oxford Street, and on his return he was greeted like a conquering hero. More importantly, his American triumph had led to a contract with a major record company there, MCA Records. Their proposals involved intensive negotiations, in much of which I assisted Dick James during his meetings in London with the executives who flew over from California for this purpose. The outcome was a contract that included million-dollar advances; but to achieve agreement on all points the Americans had to endure some of Dick's eccentricities while doing business. A particular source of irritation was his habit of taking calls on his private line notwithstanding the fact that he was in the middle of discussing an agreement which could be the basis of immense profit to both sides. The phone would ring and it would be his wife, Frances, who had a complaint over the condition of some curtains which had been returned from the cleaners to their flat in an unsatisfactory state.

Dick then had to call the cleaners to arrange for them to pick them up, indicating at the same time that he was not prepared to pay for the re-cleaning. There would then follow wrangling with the manager of the cleaners, threats to take the matter up with head office, and reporting back to Frances James. All the while, the American executives would be grinding their teeth with impatience but Dick had his own ideas about his priorities in life and both deals, the million-dollar record contract and the cleaning of the curtains, were settled to the satisfaction of all parties – except perhaps the cleaners.

Dick James realized that he had to protect his investment in his major artist. He therefore proposed to renegotiate the three contracts with Elton John, management, publishing and recording. He told Elton that he, Elton, should retain a lawyer to represent him in the negotiations. Elton, then unversed in such matters, said "Can't I use yours?" "No", said Dick, "You need to find one of your own to look after your interests". "But I don't know any lawyers", said Elton. They both then turned to me and asked if I could help. I thought I could and shortly afterwards introduced Elton to my own solicitor, Michael Oliver, an old friend who I knew had a number of clients in the entertainment world, some of them, such as the film director John Schlesinger, quite famous. Michael was at first reluctant to take on as a client a pop singer who was not then well-known at home, but after I introduced them at a first consultation they hit it off. Subsequently, Michael Oliver did an excellent job negotiating on Elton's behalf and protecting his interests in very many ways.

At another meeting in Dick James's office Elton said that he wanted to buy a flat in a quite prestigious modern block called the Water Gardens, in Tottenham Court Road. By that time he could of course afford to move away from his mother's home in Pinner to such accommodation, but he was still nervous of dealing with the somewhat up-market estate agents, Chestertons. I therefore volunteered to go with him to a meeting at their offices. They were clearly not impressed by Elton, who was even then not what could be described as a conservative dresser and, in addition, he was not by then famous in the circles in which these agents moved. Consequently, considerable doubts were raised as to his acceptability as a purchaser of the lease of the flat at the Water Gardens. Elton was disappointed and I was angry on his behalf. I reported back to Dick James, who in turn contacted his own solicitor, Teddy Barnes, a senior partner in the City firm, Stephenson Harwood & Tatham. Teddy Barnes knew top people at Chestertons, a quiet word or two was spoken and Elton got his nice new flat. I doubt if Sir Elton has such difficulties nowadays in acquiring his many properties.

Dick James had an American subsidiary company, Dick James Music Inc, which was administered in New York by Walter Hofer, my old friend from NEMS days (Dick had originally introduced him to Brian Epstein), and later on by his associate Bob Casper. DJM Inc had no staff directly employed, the necessary work of licensing recordings as the American publisher and generally looking after the Dick James interests being carried out by the attorneys, Walter, and later Bob, and by their staff in the law offices. Although this was not a structure that would be familiar in London it worked well enough, and there was constant communication between the London and New York offices. However, one of my most welcome duties was to visit the New York office, generally twice a year, to resolve in person any matters that needed direct discussion and to keep an eye on things generally. On one or two occasions my visit coincided with an American tour by Elton John. I remember in particular going to see him at a performance in Waco, Texas. I had, I think, to arrange new terms for his accompanying musicians, a chore which Elton preferred not to have to deal with himself. It was a pleasure to see him in such a place – later notorious for the FBI's massacre of the Branch Davidian sect – and his performance was as terrific as ever.

Dick James was a realist, and he knew that he was not really cut out to be a pop star's manager, nor did he wish to involve himself in the many aspects of the star's life and career which the modern manager has to handle in order to earn his keep – and retain his client. To some extent Dick resolved the problem by designating one of his employees, Steve Brown, an intense, knowledgeable and fiercely loyal fellow, to look after Elton's interests within the company, and this he did to both Elton's and Dick's satisfaction. However, the contracts with the Dick James companies were due to run out within the next twelve months or so. It was known that Elton had a friend, a very close friend, who worked at EMI Records and was interested in a professional association with him. He was very ambitious, too. His name was John Reid, a Scot who had come to London from Paisley, near Glasgow, to earn his fortune in the music business. His relationship with Elton John, both business and personal, was to be the key to his achieving his ambition.

Dick James invited John Reid to his office and after discussion agreed to employ him, on a fairly ordinary salary, specifically to look after Elton John and generally to carry out the functions of a hands-on manager on Dick's behalf. Dick made no bones, to me at any rate, about his realization that when each of Elton's contracts for management, recording and publishing fell in – which as it happened would be on different dates some months apart – John Reid would take over, first of all as manager. Thereafter, in that capacity he, John, would handle the negotiations for new lucrative contracts with major record and publishing companies.

I first met John Reid in the DJM offices, where I found him perfectly charming and clearly anxious to make a good impression. Later on, I encountered him a few times out of the office, in social situations, when the extent of his involvement in all aspects of Elton's life rapidly became apparent. They shared the flat in the Water Gardens and later the house that Elton bought in Virginia Water.

John Reid set up his own business, John Reid Enterprises with offices in Soho, and in building up his staff raided Dick James Music luring away a number of key employees. Among them was Steve Brown, one of Elton's closest allies there, and who thereafter continued to help John Reid in carrying out the management functions for which John had set up the business. In due course, we at DJM learned that John did indeed handle new contractual arrangements for Elton, which then involved in addition the Rocket companies which were formed by the two of them, and which licensed Elton's activities to major record and publishing organizations.

Dick James was good to me during the seven years which I spent working for him. Annual raises in salary were generally satisfactory, the company Jaguar I had for my exclusive use, with all expenses paid, was a source of pleasure to me and envy to others, and best of all I enjoyed working for a company that was successful in its field. When Dick James Music won the first Queens Award for Export Achievement granted to any company principally involved in pop music, I joined in the celebrations and the award ceremony held at the office. (There was some bad feeling arising from the fact that Elton and John Reid were not invited, despite the fact that it was Elton's record sales, in the United States and elsewhere, which were very largely responsible for the foreign income which formed the basis of the award. But Dick insisted that the celebratory lunch was for his family and employees only.) Dick himself went to a winners' reception at Buckingham Palace and, intensely patriotic, told me of his disgust at fellow captains of industry arriving in their Mercedes limousines. Dick of course went in his Rolls Royce, then of wholly British manufacture and ownership.

FIELD MARSHAL SIR GERALD TEMPLER, DICK JAMES AND GEOFFREY ELLIS AT THE CEREMONY HELD AT THE DJM OFFICE AT WHICH SIR GERALD, THEN LORD LIEUTENANT OF LONDON, HANDED TO DICK JAMES THE CERTIFICATE OF THE QUEEN'S AWARD FOR EXPORT ACHIEVEMENT

After Elton John's departure from the DJM fold things seemed a little flat. Dick himself maintained his enthusiasm for the business and was confident that he would discover another star among his stable of songwriters. On the law of averages this did appear unlikely since he had – in his eyes at any rate – 'discovered' Lennon & McCartney and then Elton John. To my genuine surprise, John Reid approached me out of the blue and suggested that I join his organization in my by then habitual role of Chief Administrator; American, and increasingly British, music companies would call the job Head of Business Affairs. John also invited me to be his co-director. At about the same time, Dick James, unaware of the approach by John Reid, offered me a directorship, the first outside his immediate family, together with an attractive increase in salary. After seven years with DJM I plumped for John Reid Enterprises.

I was not able to tell Dick that I was leaving until the arrangements with John Reid had been finalized. At the time I had an assistant at DJM, David Hockman, a young barrister who had forsaken the bar and had joined the company on the recommendation of Brian Sommerville, likewise a barrister, who had been Brian Epstein's and the Beatles' press officer at the time of their first visit to New York and who when I met him had incurred Brian Epstein's disfavor by his large meals from room service at the Plaza Hotel. David Hockman, who had been at DJM for some two years, came to me one morning in evident embarrassment to tell me that he was leaving, having received an attractive offer from the major music company Polygram. I was able to confound him by telling him that I too was departing from the DJM fold. David, a delightful and charming man, subsequently achieved great success in building up Polygram's music publishing arm from scratch. We are still good friends and he is now head of a major worldwide music publishing entity, operating out of New York.

14
Back In The USSR

By the time I joined John Reid Enterprises the company had moved from its rather grotty offices in Soho to a far more pleasant suite just off Grosvenor Square, in the heart of Mayfair. It was easy for me to become acquainted with the staff since the core of them had preceded me from DJM. With Dick James himself I remained on friendly terms. I suspected at first that he wanted to remain friendly since I was, so to speak, by now in the enemy's camp; but I realised in due course that he and I retained a mutual respect and later my continued relationship with him, nurtured over occasional lunches, was distinctly helpful to me.

At John Reid Enterprises I had a good rapport with the professional advisors, Barry Lyons, Elton's accountant, and of course Michael Oliver, my own solicitor, whom I had introduced to Elton. The perennial problems arising from high taxation were always present, and on an early occasion Michael, Barry and I approached, at John Reid's request, one or two high-flying City firms for advice, very little of which it must be said was worth following. One meeting was held at the City offices of Lazards. Their team deployed to meet us was led by a young lordling. Their proposals were for once interesting but I never heard that they followed them up. We felt that with such apparent lack of interest in prospective clients we on our part would not pursue the matter in that quarter. I was reminded of Peat Marwick Mitchell's turning down the Beatles and Brian Epstein as clients some years earlier.

In time, John Reid, himself never the easiest of clients, decided that he and Elton John had outgrown Barry Lyons and his small North London firm, B.H. Lyons & Co. Barry was in New York along with John Reid, Michael Oliver and myself, for discussions with American record companies, publishers and other business contacts. Before a meeting held in John's suite in the Waldorf Towers Barry told us that he had to leave during the meeting to catch a flight back to London to deal with some unexpected urgent business there. John had the use of a limousine at his disposal during his stay in New York and he politely offered it to Barry to take him to JFK airport. As soon as Barry, having gratefully accepted this offer, left, John announced to the rest of us that he was going to dispense with Barry's services as soon as he returned to London. Rather a stab in the back, I felt.

In place of Barry Lyons's firm we instructed the then leading accountancy firm, Arthur Andersen & Co. Unlike the other professionals I have mentioned they were eager to take us on as clients. The lunches they served in the top floor suite of their modern offices overlooking the River Thames, replete with butlers and fine wines were, I think, the best business lunches I have eaten.

The partner at Arthur Andersen assigned to us was Julian Lee, a larger than life figure in every sense. Immensely hard working and ebullient, he embraced his new clients with gusto. I went with him to Paris to introduce him to Elton John, who at the time was spending a substantial amount of time in a spacious flat in Neuilly. The meeting went well and Julian and I treated ourselves to dinner in a Michelin-starred restaurant. Julian and I subsequently flew together to America, and although we were in Business Class with its reasonably wide seats I felt that he might well have reserved two for himself.

In London we embarked on another round of consultations with tax counsel. One of these was Peter Rees, QC, MP. A small man, with owlish spectacles, he said in response to a complex question, "At this point, I look round wildly." In fact, his eyes, behind his glasses, moved a couple of millimeters to the left and then a couple of millimeters to the right. A short time after our consultation he had to retire from giving advice on tax avoidance as he joined the (conservative) government as a treasury minister. Later still, he became Lord Rees.

Elton was by now enjoying his prosperity and already making himself known as a lavish, and be it said generous, spender. A few days before Christmas he arrived at the John Reid office with a large cardboard box being carried by a minion. He had previously made it known that he was not going to make any effort that particular Christmas, so we were all surprised when he proceeded to unload from the box a small package for every single member of the staff. All the gifts were from Cartier in Bond Street, where he had been on a spending spree. Most people, including myself, received a Cartier watch, while a few of the very juniors got a handsome wallet. In thanking him for my gift I reminded him of his earlier decision to ignore Christmas, to which he replied "Well, its so easy at Cartier's; they've got everything I wanted and they wrap it all up nicely for you". He had by then bought his mansion near Windsor, the first of numerous seriously expensive properties, all of which he enjoyed fitting out, furnishing and decorating.

All this was some years before John Reid fell out with Elton John and they were still on the best of terms, their friendship still strong. It was some time before I realized that John, always fairly brusque and frequently short-tempered, was living life to the full, and that his lateness to work and quite frequent inattention to important meetings and details were the result of over-indulgence in alcohol and pills. Shades of Brian Epstein, although John was eventually able to overcome his demons. An occasion I remember all too well was when I, with our professional advisors, was attending a conference with yet another senior tax counsel in his chambers. In the middle of a discussion of abstruse points of tax law a nervous junior tapped

GEOFFREY ELLIS, LEFT, WITH BERNIE TAUPIN, LYRICIST, RON WHITE, HEAD OF EMI MUSIC PUBLISHING, ELTON JOHN AND JOHN REID, IN THE LATTER'S OFFICE AT THE SIGNING BY ELTON AND BERNIE OF A NEW PUBLISHING CONTRACT WITH EMI

on the door, put his head in, to the annoyance of counsel, and asked, "Is there a Mr Ellis here? Mr Reid wants him on the phone". The conference drew to a close shortly afterwards and I duly called John. He had as I knew returned that morning from Los Angeles. In a rage, he told me that he had sacked the whole staff. It transpired that due to a misunderstanding his long-suffering chauffeur, Gary Hampshire, had not met him at the airport and he had taken a taxi straight to South Audley Street, where he had managed to find fault with everyone he encountered. He had therefore ordered them all into the street, a move that attracted the attention of at least one tabloid newspaper.

I was to go to the office to make sure everyone was out. "We can do the royalty statements ourselves, with just our secretaries", said John, "and we don't need anyone else". (Patent nonsense.) I found the telephonist, desperate not to leave her busy switchboard unattended, cowering under her desk. I assured her, and the one or two remaining staff on the pavement outside, that we would be in touch with them; and over the next few days all the staff returned to the office. No more was said of the incident.

On another occasion the need arose for me to consult in person with John Reid, at a time when he was spending some months in the company's office in Los Angeles (located in a small street off Sunset Boulevard evocatively named Kings Road). I took with me some contracts and other documents that needed discussion and in some instances John's signature. Elton was on tour in California at the time, and I was hardly surprised to find on arrival at my hotel a message to the effect that Mr Reid was unable to see me as arranged that day. The next morning I found that he had left for San Francisco, where Elton was based for the time being. I dutifully followed, only to discover that by the time I arrived he had gone with Elton to his concert in Sacramento that evening. I went along with some members of the touring party who had not been accommodated on Elton's hired plane. At last I had my meeting with an affable John Reid at the stadium during the performance: we had our discussion under the bleachers, hence beneath the shrieking audience. I think we managed to make some sense. Afterwards, I was able to get on the plane for the return trip to San Francisco. On the trip Elton, who was always courteous to me – and still is, on the rare occasions when we meet these days – got up from the bunk at the back of the plane where he was resting and expressed surprise and pleasure at seeing me there. His surprise was nothing to my own at having whirled around California for the sake of a few minutes' meeting with John. At any rate, my journey from London had not been entirely wasted.

In 1977 I was co-opted on to the Entertainments Sub-Committee of the Queen's Silver Jubilee Appeal, together with such luminaries as Bernard, now Lord, Delfont, and Joyce Grenfell, under the chairmanship of the leading artists' manager and festival organizer, Sir Ian Hunter. Another member was a good friend of mine, Alan Tillotson, and he had proposed me as someone to represent the pop music world on the committee. As well as helping the other members with various projects, my own contributions included persuading Dick James to publish a song book containing hits from each of the twenty-five years of the Queen's reign. In fact, Dick, an ardent royalist, took little persuading; but he himself had some difficulties in arranging with various other publishers of the songs included to forego their royalties on sales for the benefit of the Appeal. My other major contribution consisted in arranging with John Reid for Elton John to mount a performance in aid of the Appeal, which took place at The Rainbow, a somewhat run down North London venue which was a converted cinema. It was attended by Her Royal Highness Princess Alexandra and her husband, the Hon. Angus Ogilvy. The princess sat between John Reid and me in the front row of the circle and appeared to enjoy the show, though seeming a little uncertain whether to clap along with most of the audience to some of Elton's more rousing numbers, as John did, or to appear more restrained like myself. The evening raised the expected large sum for the Appeal. It made at least one tabloid headline the next day since Princess Alexandra had, in congratulating Elton backstage after the performance, asked him whether, to sustain the energy he displayed on stage, he needed some sort of stimulant. It was reputed at the time that Elton was indulging in a different type of stimulant than that which the princess had in mind.

I had another brush with royalty when, John Reid being as so often abroad, I represented the company at a dinner given to thank supporters of a visit to the Royal Opera House, Covent Garden, by the New York City Ballet. We had agreed to help to promote this venture and my fellow guests at the dinner included the heads of various enterprises, oil companies, banks and others, with their spouses. I took an old friend, Judy Gibson, and we arrived on time for the dinner held at Les Ambassadeurs Club, in Hamilton Place. The guest of Honor was Her Royal Highness The Princess Margaret. She was late, and we all stood around drinking champagne while awaiting her arrival. Eventually she swept in with a group of her own friends with whom she then chatted, while herself having a few drinks. After a time her equerry came up to me and proposed that I should be presented to her, as a means of breaking up her jolly little circle. I was at the time chatting with a pleasant American woman, the wife of an oil executive, and we were hurried over to the princess. After we had been presented by name, and made our bobs, she said nothing. So I, emboldened by a few glasses, did the unforgivable and spoke first, uttering some such banality as "What a splendid occasion, ma'am". She simply stared at me, still saying nothing, and then looked away; we shambled off, embarrassed. The princess was clearly having a bad day, or evening, as on being told of the menu for dinner, lovingly prepared by the club's renowned chef, she simply said, "Can I have something different?" Not a happy occasion.

It had an odd sequel for me. A few weeks later I went to a charity lunch in the country in aid of the Silver Jubilee Appeal, organized by my old friend on the Entertainments Sub-Committee, Alan Tillotson. Princess Margaret was coming and I was again at the last moment dragooned into the line-up of people to be presented. "Heavens", I thought to myself, "She's going to say, there's that dreadful man who spoke to me". But all passed off without a hitch this time and the princess was all sweetness and light.

One day I was beavering away in my office at John Reid Enterprises when the receptionist buzzed me to tell me that an American lady had arrived unannounced to see John Reid, who was once more abroad. It was urgent and important and would I please see her in his stead. She came in and I at once recognized her as the film star Faye Dunaway. She was accompanied by her boyfriend, the photographer Terry O'Neil. She apologized for appearing without prior warning – although her appearance was in fact a most welcome distraction – and explained that she was interested in buying John Reid's house, which was indeed a most attractive property in Montpelier Square, one of London's most prestigious locations. He had bought it from a friend of mine, Julian Gibbs, a few years earlier; it seemed that he had mentioned to a friend of Miss Dunaway's that in view of his very frequent and lengthy absences abroad he was considering selling. I knew nothing of this and could only promise to raise the matter with John on her behalf.

When I did speak to him about this he was dismissive and I thought no more about it. However, a few days later a call came to me from Miss Dunaway's lawyer in New York; he said she was in his office there and would like to speak to me. "Oh, Mr Ellis", she cooed, "What has Mr Reid said?" I told her that he did not seem interested in selling at the moment, at which she put forward an offer that he could use her no doubt sumptuous apartment in New York if she could live for a time in the London house. Although I relayed this proposal to

John I heard no more about it. I had the niggling suspicion that she did not then have the funds for an outright purchase; but the matter did not proceed that far.

As with the Beatles, it was never part of my duties to go to the artists' concerts or to travel with them on tour. But John Reid induced me to go to Russia in 1979. In truth, I needed little persuasion, as the Soviet Union was still closed to most westerners and labored under the repressive Brezhnev regime. A deal had been negotiated for Elton John to be the first major Western pop star to perform in Leningrad – as it still was – and Moscow. The deal done with Gosconcert, the state agency and promoter, provided relatively modest remuneration by our standards, certainly by Elton's, but it supplied travel, accommodation and internal transport for twelve people. Elton and entourage consisted of nine, so his mother and stepfather, Sheila and Fred Farebrother, and I made up the numbers. We were also accompanied by two journalists, David Wigg of the Daily Express and Robert Hilburn from the Los Angeles Times; the latter had been one of the first American critics to enthuse about Elton when he had made his first US appearance at the Troubadour Club and had remained on friendly terms with him and John Reid ever since. A small film team came along as well, to make a documentary about the visit.

This trip to the USSR was clearly something of an adventure. We flew from London to Moscow on Aeroflot, the Soviet airline, which was not very comfortable. On arrival in Moscow we immediately entrained for Leningrad in a special carriage attached to the regular overnight express. It was said that this carriage was generally for the use of high officials, and it was indeed quite comfortable. There were not enough compartments for everyone in the party to have one to him or herself and there was much nervous giggling about who was sharing with whom. David Wigg made an agreeable traveling companion for me. There were attached to our party three officials from Gosconcert, two nice and helpful young women who both had a reasonable command of English, and a tall, very handsome man named Sacha, whose function was not apparent; some maintained that he was from the secret police, assigned to keep an eye on us and make sure no-one stepped out of line. He was friendly but somewhat aloof, with little English.

The hotel in Leningrad was large and dreary. The hotel restaurant, where we had all our meals, served meat, fish or fowl, not otherwise described and which all tasted the same. Meals were washed down with a sweet champagne-style wine. The concert hall where Elton performed was however modern, with excellent facilities. The audiences, drawn we were told from approved families and schools and on their best behavior, were at first quiet and respectful; but Elton soon roused them to the same sort of enthusiasm which his performances always induced in Europe and America. At one point in the first concert he kicked away the piano stool and continued playing his rock 'n' roll number standing up. The organizers asked him not to do that again – damaging Soviet property – but he continued to do so, making it part of the act.

Although I attended nearly all the shows – nothing else to do – I managed to do some sightseeing during the day and found Leningrad even then to be fascinating, full of beautiful buildings, some of them at that time in a dilapidated condition. I also took a trip out to Tsarkoe Selo with an English-speaking guide; it was not permitted for a foreigner to go alone. When I asked her some questions about the revolutionary period she affected to know nothing about the imprisonment there of the last Tsar, Nicholas II, and his family prior to their transportation to Siberia and their deaths. I also went to the Peterhof, some way outside Leningrad, and with one or two others on the tour attended the Kirov Ballet in their 'Coppelia', a magical experience. All this was very exciting, being years before the loosening up of travel and tourism to Soviet Russia. We all went too,

Elton included, on a tour of the vast Hermitage Museum, where the authorities specially opened for us the Treasury, full of staggering gold artefacts and jewellery, not then open to the general public.

Back in Moscow we encountered an early heat wave; it was May. The air-conditioning in our modern hotel was not very effective but, as in Leningrad, the vast concert hall, just off Red Square, was well cooled, with excellent facilities. The audience, again as in Leningrad, was clean and well dressed and, although very enthusiastic, very well behaved. It happened that a couple of months later I went to Elton's same show, this time in the Palladium, New York, a run down theatre on 14th Street, where the audience was for the most part distinctly grubby, the men with long hair and torn jeans. There was a miasma of smoke from tobacco and marijuana hanging over the audience, and I could not help comparing this atmosphere with that in the Russian concert halls. In this instance at least, the comparison was unfavorable to the capitalist West.

Elton John seemed to thrive on his Russian venture and was sociable to everyone he met there. In Leningrad, after each performance, we all gathered in the hotel's 'hard currency' bar, which the local populace was unable to penetrate. Only those with dollars, sterling or other western money to spend were admitted, and it seemed that most of the heavy drinkers there came from Finland; they could easily travel from Helsinki for a day or two of hard and cheap drinking. One night in the bar Elton confided to me that he had struck up a close friendship with the mysterious Sacha. "Good for you", I said. Later on, in Moscow, Sacha came round after the show to introduce Elton to his wife and children. Elton was somewhat taken aback.

I had a ticket to return to London half way through the Moscow week as I had much to do in the office. John Reid found out about this and, bored by then with Russia, demanded that I give up my ticket to him. I refused and we had the only stand up row I personally experienced with him. Eventually, he managed to secure a ticket on the same Aeroflot flight and we found that we were the only passengers in first class. The outburst of anger had been totally unnecessary, often the case with John.

Traveling with John and Elton was always an interesting experience. Once I went with them to America at the start of one of Elton's nationwide tours. On the Pan Am jumbo jet we made an odd party. Elton was in his customary mish-mash of clothing, topped by a baseball cap. John and I, both seasoned travelers, were in quite informal gear, certainly tieless. The most respectable member of the party was John's resident cook, Graham Carpenter, who was in a sober suit and tie. Anyone seeing the four of us at the table laid for us in the upper first class cabin would, if he did not know Elton's identity, have thought that Graham, whom John had brought along because of his distaste for post-performance snacks in American hotels, was the patron, perhaps, of an eccentric group of ageing performers.

For a fairly short period we had the group 'Queen' under management and John, during this time, secured a lucrative recording contract for them, involving the production of a specified number of LPs during the years of the contract. However, after one record had been produced John Reid fell out with the band. The result was a termination of the management agreement, but with John having cannily agreed with Jim Beach, the band's lawyer, that John Reid Enterprises would receive part of the income from all the future recordings to be produced under the contract he had negotiated for them. A useful source of income for doing nothing further.

My initial contract with John Reid Enterprises was for three years, from 1976 to 1979. At the end of this period my relationship with John remained good and the company was flourishing. We had invested in imposing offices in Lancaster Gate, overlooking Hyde Park, and John told me that he could only keep going with all the demands on him if I continued as his co-director. But at the beginning of the 1980s our relationship started going sour. Eventually, at the end of my second three years in 1982 we agreed to part. John generously allowed me to keep the Bentley which the company had bought for my use.

15
Do You Want To Know A Secret?

Quite soon after leaving John Reid Enterprises I spent six months working for a small independent publishing and recording company controlled by Gerry Bron, the brother of the actress Eleanor Bron whom I had met during the filming of 'Help!' in Salzburg and the son of Sydney Bron, the old-time music publisher for whom Dick James had worked as a song plugger on giving up his singing career. During this short time with Gerry Bron I received two significant phone calls.

The first was from an old friend in music publishing, Jim Doyle. He told me that he was working with someone else I knew, Kaplan Kaye, to produce a novelty single record. This was a take-off of the tennis star John McEnroe, whose loss of temper and swearing at the umpire had caused a sensation at the Wimbledon championships. On the record, to the background of a disco beat, a singer impersonating McEnroe was heard remonstrating with the umpire, who had ruled that "The ball was out". "Chalk dust, it was chalk dust", called the McEnroe character. The recording session had been going well enough, with the musical background in the can and the 'tennis star' performing well. But the producers could not find someone with the right kind of British voice and accent to provide a satisfactory contrast as the umpire. "Why not ask Geoffrey Ellis?" someone suggested. "He'd never do it", said the producers. "Well, try him." Jim Doyle tried me, and I was tickled pink with the idea. I duly attended at the studio, rehearsed and did my part ("The ball was out!") which included uttering the words, "Frankly, sir, you're a pain in the bum", all in the space of a few hours.

Kaplan and Jim were operating on a shoestring budget and it was to be a problem paying me a session fee, then I believe about £30, so I told them not to pay me then but to grant me a very small percentage of receipts as a royalty on sales of the record. I prepared the necessary agreement and everyone was happy. Especially me, when the record became something of a hit, reaching number 19 in the UK chart (so I could boast of being on a Top 20 Hit). It did well in a number of foreign territories as well, reaching number 1 in Belgium and, I believe, number 2 in Holland, as well as achieving good sales in Australia and South Africa. Alas, no distributor could be found for the States, so we missed out on the biggest market of all; but I eventually pocketed quite a tidy sum.

I had insisted on anonymity, with no credit on the record. I had also stipulated, at the time half in jest, that if the record, called "Chalk Dust; the Umpire Strikes Back", should be a hit, then I would not have to appear on TV on 'The Top of the Pops'. Accordingly, when the record rose into the top 20 Kaplan Kaye performed my role before the cameras. I was quite content to have been behind the microphone.

The other call I received, near the end of my time with the Bron organization, was from Dick James, with whom I still remained on good terms. He asked me to go and see him and when I did, he showed me a letter he had received from solicitors acting for Elton John and Bernie Taupin. This alleged fraud and underpayment of royalties from the songs published and the records made under the contracts with the Dick James organization. Dick, who believed passionately in his personal probity, was appalled at receiving this letter before action. He asked me, when I was free, to undertake research into the full history of Elton's and Bernie's relationship with Dick James Music and This Record Company. Dick pointed out that I was the best person to do this work since I had been present during almost the whole of the relevant period, and had in fact been involved in agreeing and preparing much of the documentation. He would of course pay me a fee based on the amount of work involved.

This offer presented me with something of a dilemma, since I had worked for both sides to the dispute; the writ swiftly ensued. On the other hand, the work would be interesting and I felt in my bones that right was on Dick James's side. He had always acted in what he perceived to be in the best interests of the artists and writers contracted to his companies. Unfortunately, it was, and is, axiomatic that almost always when pop artists achieve great success they come to resent the compensation paid to the managers, record companies and publishers who have contributed to their careers, often at considerable initial outlay. The point was proved when, years later, John Reid, who was the guiding force behind Elton John's action against Dick James, was himself at the receiving end of legal action by Elton.

I agreed to carry out the research required by Dick James and his lawyers, and fairly wearisome and time-consuming this turned out to be. My own solicitor prepared an undertaking for me to sign in which I agreed not to use any information I had gleaned while working for John Reid Enterprises, and this was supplied to Elton's legal team. In fact, respecting this undertaking caused me no difficulty since the current action concerned the effects of contracts entered into long before I joined John Reid's organization.

The detailed – very detailed – writ which was served on Dick James Music, This Record Company and Dick James personally (the last to his considerable outrage) required payment of large sums of additional royalties, over and above of course the enormous sums already paid over the years, and the return to Elton and Bernie of copyright in all the songs written by them while they were under contract to DJM.

Eventually, after well over a year's preparatory work, the case came to trial in the High Court in London. Numerous legal luminaries appeared: for Dick James, George Newman QC, later a High Court judge, assisted by Stephen Silber, later a QC and then some years on himself a High Court judge. Elton John's leading counsel was Mark Littman QC, an establishment figure who sat on the boards of several prominent companies and was said to undertake little litigation work at the time. We learned that Mr Littman had been in America when Elton John achieved his initial breakthrough success there and had been greatly impressed on attending a performance by his future client. Curiously, he is referred to twice by the late American artist Andy Warhol in his published diaries as 'the Queen of England's lawyer', although this is a distinction I have not seen recorded elsewhere. The diarist James Lees-Milne writes that he (Mr Littman) was 'said to be the cleverest lawyer alive'.

The judge was Mr Justice Nicholls, now Lord Nicholls of Birkenhead, a Lord of Appeal in Ordinary.

The hearing lasted for many weeks and I attended nearly every day. A great deal of time was taken up by examination of documents and enquiry into the circumstances of their negotiation. All the principals, it seemed to me, acquitted themselves well although Dick James, against his counsel's advice, took advantage of his time in the witness box to sound off about the injustice of the case; and Bernie Taupin, who had come from his home in California to give evidence, clearly remembered nothing at all about the contracts which had enabled him to become a rich man. The judge was clearly fascinated by Elton John, to whom he was particularly courteous.

Mr Littman's technique included throwing the other side's witnesses off balance at the start of his cross-examination. When Dick James's son Stephen, who had responsibility for much of the record company's operation, was exposed to questioning by him Mr Littman started out by asking some apparently innocuous questions about the renegotiation of a record distribution contract in Japan which Stephen had carried out. This had little apparent relevance to the matters in hand but counsel, by his probing questions, was able to show that there had been considerable confusion over the statistics which Stephen had used in securing higher royalties than before. Turning then to matters more important to the case he had a witness who was by then to some extent thrown off balance.

When my own turn came to start two-and-a-half days in the box, Mr Littman, who had done his homework very thoroughly, referred to my Oxford law degree and asked me some fairly basic questions about aspects of the contracts in contention for which I had some responsibility. It was not an altogether comfortable experience, but I doubt if anything I said in evidence swayed the judge one way or another.

The outcome of the case was something of a compromise. The judge ordered the payment of substantial extra backdated royalties, to Dick James's dismay, but rejected the allegations of fraud and refused to order the return of copyrights in the songs and recordings to Elton and Bernie. When I congratulated Dick and counsel on the latter they were not impressed, being more concerned at the time with the financial aspects. Nevertheless, I believe I was right to consider the retention of copyrights as being of the greater importance. A few years later, after Dick James's death from a heart attack brought on, some believe, largely by the stress of the action, Stephen James was able to sell the company, complete with the Elton John and Bernie Taupin copyrights, for a sum vastly in excess of what it would have been worth without them. The purchaser was PolyGram International Music Publishing, the deal being negotiated by its then Managing Director, David Hockman, who had worked with me at DJM a number of years earlier.

EPILOGUE
When I'm Sixty-Four

A few years ago I accepted an invitation to attend as a Special Guest a 'Beatlefest' to be held at a hotel in Secaucus, New Jersey, some miles outside New York City. I had known of these events for sometime and my interest had recently been aroused by the late Ray Coleman, a journalist and the biographer of John Lennon and Brian Epstein among others in the pop music world. He had himself attended a number of Beatlefests, all in the USA, and had written entertainingly and informatively about them and their organizer, Mark Lapidos, in the London Sunday Times. These conventions, each attracting several thousand Beatle fans, were held three times a year, in or near New York, Chicago and Los Angeles. I discussed them with Ray Coleman and the upshot was the invitation to me to attend, as the advance publicity stated, "Beatlefest '95, N.Y. Metro's 25th Official Beatles' Fan's (sic) Celebration!!!" There had up until then been twenty-four such events in the New York area and over the years more than seventy throughout America. Similar conventions have been held elsewhere, for instance in Toronto, but these were not under the auspices of Mr Lapidos, himself a dyed-in-the-wool Beatles fan and a shrewd businessman. He was however thinking of branching out and was at the time considering holding a trial Beatlefest in Tokyo.

I set off from Heathrow Airport in company with two other Special Guests from England, Pauline Sutcliffe, the sister of Stuart Sutcliffe, the original Beatle who died at the age of twenty-two before the group became famous; and Alan Clayson, a slightly wild character whose career has included performing as a musician, pop music journalism and writing books about George Harrison and Ringo Starr. He and Pauline Sutcliffe, who in real life runs an art gallery in London, had collaborated in the writing of 'Backbeat', a book derived from the film of the same name which told the story of Stuart Sutcliffe and the Beatles.

On arrival at John F. Kennedy Airport in New York we were met by a stretch limousine replete with dark windows, drinks cabinet (empty) and TV set (inoperative). After arriving at the Meadowlands Hilton Hotel where the Beatlefest was to take place over the following three days and where we were all accommodated, we were joined at dinner with Mark Lapidos by the remaining Special Guests: Louise Harrison, the sister of George; Angie McCartney, who in 1964 had married Paul's widowed father, thus becoming his stepmother (when he was already famous), and her daughter by her previous marriage, Ruth. She, Paul's stepsister, had taken the family name and as Ruth McCartney was herself pursuing a career as a singer. For reasons which I could not determine she was at the time concentrating her efforts in Russia, where she had performed in many cities with great success. Louise, Angie, who was widowed in 1976, and Ruth all lived in America and seemed to have absorbed that country's ebullience and enthusiasm for life.

During our dinner conversation Mr Lapidos remarked that if anyone present didn't love all the Beatles' music he or she might as well go home. It was only a light-hearted remark but it made me feel a little guilty, as I have never in truth been a whole-hearted lover of all the Beatles' music, or indeed a fan of pop music as a whole.

The Beatlefest was to be held over a weekend, on Friday, Saturday and Sunday. When we arrived on Thursday the Hilton presented a perfectly normal appearance, but by the next day many of the internal decorations had been removed: mirrors had been taken down from the corridor walls and flowers and plants, even artificial ones, had disappeared from the public rooms, giving them a rather bleak appearance. In the bar all drinks over the weekend were sold in plastic cups rather than the normal glasses in which we had been served the day before. These precautions against rowdy behavior proved quite unnecessary as the Beatles fans were not at all aggressive in manner and there were no signs of excessive drinking or rowdyism. They took over the whole hotel and the only activity that could have been considered at all anti-social was the constant playing of music, both recorded and live, during waking hours. This was generally at very high volume, but since it was practically all Beatles music it was welcome to the conventioneers and there were no other hotel guests to be bothered by it. At the end of the week the hotel's management confirmed that there had been not a single untoward incident or complaint.

The printed Beatlefest programme carried a prominent photograph of me, heading the Special Guests, and I was described as "...one of those rare and few Beatles insiders that has never spoken about his experiences before". The blurb continued: "Geoffrey was a close friend of Brian Epstein and co-Director of NEMS Enterprises from 1964-1968. After Brian died, he worked with Dick James, the original publisher of the Lennon/McCartney treasure of songs. We thank our good friend Ray Coleman for putting Geoffrey in touch with us. We are sure he will be a truly 'special' guest".

Special or not, I had not been told in advance precisely what was expected of me in return for Mark Lapidos's having transported me from England and accommodated me in some comfort. The programme revealed that the fest was to take place from 5.30pm on the Friday until 12.30am, from 12 noon to midnight on Saturday and from noon till 11pm on Sunday. On Friday I and the other Specials were billed to appear all together on the stage of the Grand Ballroom at 7pm for a ninety-minute session in which we would be interviewed by a New York disc jockey and subjected to questions from the audience; the ballroom had a seating capacity of over a thousand. At 10pm we were scheduled for another hour of an 'Informal Q & A Session' in a smaller room holding a hundred or so. On the Saturday I had a solo spot of an hour with a disc jockey, Jimmy Fink, interviewing me in the Grand Ballroom, and was to participate with others in the smaller room for an hour and a half at 8.30 in 'General Discussions and Autograph Session'. And on the final day I had 50 minutes starting at 3.30 with Mr Fink before the Grand Ballroom audience and, with the rest, an open-ended Q & A and autograph session in the other room, starting at 5.45. On the Sunday, I was asked in addition to participate in an "Author's Forum" at 2 pm. All this sounded fairly daunting, particularly since I and the other Specials were urged to put ourselves about and be available for informal meetings with fans for the full duration of the fest.

The programme gave details of the many other sessions and activities of the weekend. There were endless showings of tapings of actual Beatles performances and of their feature films, 'A Hard Day's Night', 'Help!', 'Let It Be' and the full-length animated cartoon 'Yellow Submarine', as well as of the series of half-hour cartoons made for children's TV which had preceded the making of that film. There were auctions of memorabilia, a sound-alike contest (for the best imitation of the Beatles) and a 'Beatlefest Recording Studio' in which fans could pretend they were the Beatles, singing to instrumental tracks. The words of the songs were helpfully shown on a video screen, but the fans knew them all anyway. There was an enormous Beatles' Marketplace, selling all sorts of merchandise, from tee-shirts to books (over 100 Beatles-related publications), from ties to posters and from photo collections to records and videos. Many dealers, both professional and private, brought along their wares and business was very brisk. A highlight each evening was a performance by a group called 'Liverpool', who somewhat resembled the Beatles in appearance and performed amazingly like the original. They were given a terrific reception each night in a packed Grand Ballroom.

The programme stated that the Beatlefest was a Smoke Free Environment and that the programme itself was printed on 100% Recycled Paper.

Over six thousand fans attended. Some stayed in the Hilton, others in a nearby Sheraton Hotel, but the majority came for just one day's session by car and bus. Tickets cost from $14 for the Friday session and $19 for Saturday or Sunday; or $42 for all three days, with half-price for children under nine (free for under-fives). Special buses came from Manhattan, charging $12 return.

The fans, without exception were friendly and polite, mostly seemed to be in their twenties and thirties, with a very few over forty. Some parents brought small children, who were thus in training to become the next generation of Beatles fans. Few if any of those attending could have seen the Beatles live: they stopped performing live as a group in 1967, nearly thirty years earlier. Indeed, of the very many who spoke to me, in public or privately, none said that they had actually seen the Beatles. They were therefore genuinely in awe of someone who had actually known them thirty years ago. It struck me that there was quite a large number of people who might politely be termed disadvantaged, by physical, or in a few instances, mild mental problems. Mark Lapidos told me that a local nursing home had in fact arranged transport for a busload of inmates to attend one day. The common characteristic of everyone was happiness and enthusiasm, and it was clear that being a Beatles fan was an important, indeed integral, part of their lives, in many cases perhaps a therapeutic part.

Initially I felt somewhat out of place. Since I was by then in my sixties I was considerably older than everyone else, both organizers and visiting fans. Also, I am generally most comfortable, at any rate at work or in public, wearing shirt and tie, whereas everyone else was in casual clothing. I was afraid people would think I was not entering into the spirit of the occasion. But no one seemed to mind and I met nothing but friendliness and interest all round.

I was nervous too about my appearances before the audiences of fans, both alone and with the other Specials. No set speech was expected, but I had scribbled some notes of topics I could talk about and a few fairly anodyne anecdotes I could relate. I had made it clear to Mark Lapidos before coming to America that I would not be prepared to discuss what knowledge I might have had of the sex lives of the Beatles or those near to them; nor would I talk about drugs and any alleged effects that they might have had in the past. Mark assured me that these topics were extremely unlikely to arise and in the event this proved true. While I was asked a few serious questions about business aspects of the Beatles' careers, such as the song publishing arrangements and the vexed question of merchandising rights, mostly the fans asked such questions as what did Brian Epstein do as their manager and why did the Beatles after his death not give him more credit. (Why indeed?) Also, what was my opinion of the propriety of the three surviving Beatles then currently resurrecting a partly finished song, the thirty year old tape which had John Lennon singing on it, as a forthcoming 'new' release on which all four would now be heard performing? A tricky question, this, on which everyone but me seemed to have strong views. The nearest my questioners came to intimate personal details was when I was asked, predictably, whether Brian Epstein had committed suicide. Even then, when I gave an emphatic denial, citing the coroner's verdict of accidental death, the question of Brian's sexuality was not raised.

It dawned on me, in fact, that the fans really had no interest in any unpleasant or controversial aspects of the lives and activities of the Beatles and those close to them. They simply loved the music and revered the Beatles as musicians, entertainers and beings far beyond their ken. One interesting question that was raised was why was there still so much more evident enthusiasm for them in America than there was, the fans believed, in Britain. Not really knowing the answer, I had to fall back on the difference in national characteristics, with the British, crowded on our small island, more concerned to defend our space and not interfere with others' privacy; while Americans, with all the space they need and their natural exuberance, find it easier to express their feelings of enthusiasm in the present instance and presumably of hatred when appropriate. (The only booing I heard during the sessions was when the name of Allen Klein was mentioned: an American accountant and manager, he had come into the Beatles' lives after Brian Epstein's death, and his activities and eventual disgrace in their eyes had made him into a hate figure for the fans.)

At any rate I received a gratifying measure of applause at the end of each of my appearances and was dogged by autograph hunters both then and while I was walking or chatting in the corridors or meeting rooms. I took care to point out many times that my signature was worthless, but that did not deter the fans and I duly signed, mostly over my photograph in the programme. One fan brought me eight programmes to be signed, each one to be dedicated to a different relative. All in all, I must have signed several hundred and have as a result great sympathy for the truly famous for whom this must be an unbearable chore. I was later told by an acquaintance who had been a Special guest at several Beatlefests that there is in fact a market for our autographs: he had found his own listed for sale at $5. I don't think I want to know how much my own signature was worth, but perhaps the young lady with eight of them was able to cover the cost of her attendance.

I was particularly interested in the sessions involving the authors of a number of new Beatles-related books. They were there to publicize these to an obvious market and were able to present them to an audience of the fans at two 'Authors' Forums'. Among the new publications whose authors discussed them there was one comprising solely a listing of Beatles records and their prices in Japan; another book consisted of a detailed hour by hour account of the day, July 6, 1957, when John Lennon met Paul McCartney, 'a significant day in Beatles' history'; there was a new in-depth history of the great 1969 'Paul is Dead' hoax; a Memorabilia Price Guide; and an 'Unauthorized Story of the Beatles Get Back Sessions 1964'. These books, curious though I found some of them, were all fairly innocuous and did nothing to harm the Beatles' reputation. Mark Lapidos told me that he was careful to ensure that publications featured at the fests were not in any way damaging. He cited the instance of a book that had gained wide publicity on its publication in 1983. It had been co-written by a former NEMS and Apple employee who had for a time been quite close to the Beatles, with an American journalist who had a sensational writing style. The book purported to reveal among other things secrets of the Beatles' marital and other affairs, initially, Mr Lapidos, believing that it had been written with Beatles' approval, had featured it at the next Beatlefest; but when he discovered that this was not the case and that they were dismayed at their former confidant's having written it he had it removed from display and sale.

As well as the books mentioned, there were a number of other new publications being presented by their authors, and of particular interest to me was one that centered on an analysis of discarded sound tapes from original Beatles' recording sessions that EMI Records retains in its archives. My interest was not so much in the author's consideration of this material as in the background to the tapes in question. In his presentation to the audience he referred to the difficulties he had encountered in gaining access to the tapes. The surviving Beatles, Paul, George and Ringo, with Mrs Yoko Lennon, their Apple organization and the legal representatives of all of them are assiduous in guarding the privacy of such material; but the author of this new book, an apparently serious investigative journalist, had gone direct to EMI Records and had succeeded in securing access to the tapes, although he admitted his belief that had the EMI executives concerned consulted the parties mentioned above – as perhaps they should have done – he might well have been refused permission. In the event, he had covered his back by securing the services of the legal staff of the New Yorker magazine, for which he had written (as it happens a profile of Mark Lewisohn, said to be the greatest living expert on the Beatles) and they had given assurances that publication of the book, based on the hidden tapes, could go ahead.

The author maintained that the public had a right to know all about these tapes and to hear them, whatever the attitude of the artists, their creators, might be. I pointed out that there had been cases, certainly in the UK, wherein successful pop artists had been able to prevent the release by their record companies of early tapes, although the companies arguably had the contractual right to do so, on the grounds that availability of such recordings to the public would be detrimental to their careers, being raw, unfinished or otherwise unsatisfactory to the artists. The present author would have none of this. He stated that the importance of the Beatles in the history of the twentieth century was such as to override all such niceties and to make access to all aspects of their artistic career imperative. He drew the startling analogy of the Nixon tapes, which were made available to the public under US Federal Law during Nixon's lifetime, despite the fact that this was the last thing the former president wanted. I found it hard to swallow this argument.

Many of those present at the Beatlefest, among both my fellow guests and the attendant fans, asked me why I had not written my own book. They did not accept my explanations of a decent – I hope – reticence and a busy career, encompassing participation later in the management of, among others, Elton John, and finally a senior executive position with the Performing Right Society. I was urged to write my own recollections, which I hope will in the event prove at least as interesting as 'The Japanese Record Price Guide 1994'.

GEOFFREY ELLIS

Another title from Thorogood

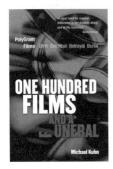

ONE HUNDRED FILMS AND A FUNERAL

Michael Kuhn

£19.99 • Cased • ISBN: 1 85418 216 1

The meteoric rise of PolyGram Films, producer of Four Weddings and a Funeral, the first real British challenge to Hollywood, and its equally dramatic demise.

"Michael Kuhn is a visionary who created the most successful global film company outside of Hollywood... He failed, of course, but he very nearly pulled it off. Kuhn's candid firsthand account of PolyGram Films' success and demise is a must read for anyone interested in the brutally sharp end of the business of film, or anyone who ever wondered why the films emanating from the Hollywood machine are mostly crap."

SIR ALAN PARKER, FILM DIRECTOR

"I have read other books in the showbiz insider sub-genre but his is by far the best because it is matter-of-fact understated, honest and avoids both schlock-horror and self pity... Congratulations."

JAMES MURRAY, MANAGING DIRECTOR, AUSTRAL-MEDIA PTY LTD, SYDNEY